6/94

Pandas

CHRIS CATTON

For my son Joe, whose generation will be
left to clear up when the party is over.

Pandas

CHRIS CATTON

Facts On File Publications
New York, New York • Oxford, England

Facts On File, Inc.
460 Park Avenue South
New York NY 10016
USA

Library of Congress Cataloging-in-Publication Data

Catton, Chris.
  Pandas / Chris Catton.
    p.   cm.
  Includes bibliographical references.
  Summary: Relates how pandas were discovered, their habitat and behavior, and recent efforts to restore the panda's population in the wild.
  ISBN 0-8160-2331-X
  1. Giant panda.   [1. Giant Panda. 2. Pandas.]   I. Title.
QL737.C214C37   1990
599.74′443—dc20

Facts On File books are available at special discounts when purchased in bulk quantities for businesses, associations, institutions or sales promotions. Please contact the Special Sales Department of our New York office at 212/683-2244 (dial 800/322-8755 except in NY, AK or HI).

Printed in Great Britain
10 9 8 7 6 5 4 3 2 1

Contents

List of colour plates

List of figures

Acknowledgements

It is a pleasure to be able to thank everyone who has helped in making this book possible. Special thanks are due to Ip Kwok Kin, who after being thrown in at the deep end with two unsympathetic foreigners, survived to become a good interpreter and friend; to Don Reid, for his bottomless patience in answering my questions and for his careful review of much of the finished manuscript; to Ken and Jenny Johnson, for their help and encouragement, and to Tony Allen and James Gray, for their companionship and good humour in the field in conditions that were often uncomfortable and at times downright nasty. Also to Steve O'Brien, for being the first to suggest that I might be capable of writing this book.

The historical section would be very much less detailed and less accurate were it not for the very considerable help of Richard J. Reynolds III, who was kind enough to share with me his broad knowledge which results from many years of interest in the subject. I cannot thank him enough for the steady flow of letters that brightened many a dull winter morning. Erika Brady of Southeast Missouri State University kindly provided the addresses of Colonel Jack Young and his brother Quentin. I would like to thank Jack Young for providing several useful references and confirming the accuracy of published accounts of his exploits.

The current taxonomy of bamboos is in disarray, and work on bamboos relevant to this book has often been published in obscure journals. Special thanks are due to Michael Hirsh, Secretary of the European Bamboo Society, for help in tracing much relevant material.

Many researchers kindly sent me copies of reprints, or have allowed me to quote material currently in press. For this I am grateful to Angela R. Glatston, Pralad B. Yonzon, John L. Gittleman, and (again) to Don Reid. I am also grateful to the many workers in Wolong who gave freely of their time and knowledge—in particular to Dong Cai, Ouyang Gang, Chen Yen Mu, Qiu Xian Meng, Wang Xiong Qing and Lao Pen, to John MacKinnon, Rob DeWulf and the many others who have cheerfully suffered my struggle to grasp the subjects of which they are masters.

I would also like to thank Elizabeth Hallett, Zhang Yong Ning and Dong Ming for translating many papers from Chinese; Simon Blackwell and the Cotswold Wildlife Park, for freely giving information on captive red pandas and allowing me to take photographs (Plates 10, 11); Nick Allen of Wolfson College, Oxford, for his advice on the derivation of the word 'panda'; Steven Johnson, supervising librarian of the New York Zoological Society, for checking his files and confirming the fate of the animal that left China in 1946 and as far as I could discover had simply disappeared; Steve Bircher, Assistant Curator of Mammals at St Louis Zoo, for archive material on 'Happy'; and Mick Carman, for providing details of the most recent captive-born animals. Thanks are also due to the staff of the Radcliffe Science Library, the libraries of the departments of Plant Sciences and Zoology at Oxford University, the British Library and Natural History Museum Libraries, and the library of the London Zoological Society.

Thanks too to Len Bown, for careful copy-editing, and to the staff at Christopher Helm who cheerfully and efficiently turned the manuscript into a book.

Last but by no means least, I should like to thank Tony Allen, James Gray, Mick Carman, Richard Reynolds, Don Reid and Ken Johnson for reading part or all of the manuscript and making many helpful comments and suggestions.

Introduction

Last Christmas I stood in a large London department store and watched a mother trapped by the display of cuddly toys battling with her two-year-old child. 'All right then, but you can only have one', she sighed in desperation to the red and increasingly noisy face at her knee. Arms in the air and face instantly transformed into a huge grin, the child jumped up and down repeating what was probably one of only a hundred or so words it knew—'panda'.

Why is it that these animals have such a powerful grip on the human imagination? Ramona and Desmond Morris concluded their 1966 book on the giant panda with a list of 20 points which they felt might explain its appeal. We have learned a great deal about the lives of pandas in the last 20 years, but we are no closer to understanding exactly why it is that we find them so fascinating. As the Morrises suggested, the panda's popularity is probably the result of many different character-traits that appeal independently to different people and age-groups. To small children it appears cuddly and soft, suggesting comfort and security. Often it is playful, happy to climb a ladder or tree in captivity, and its clumsy movements bring a clownish humour to everything it does. Its name is short, easy to remember, and easy to say—before the arrival of the first specimens to English zoos, the panda was known for a while as the parti-coloured bear, a name which would have stood little chance of making a big hit with two-year-olds. And the panda's distinctive black and white markings and large size make it easy to identify—something that can be named with certainty in a complex and confusing world.

The panda is also high on the list of favourite animals for older children and adults. With a growing sense of right and wrong, older children find pandas attractive because they do not have to kill for their food, and because they are harmless and seem friendly. Sitting up straight to eat and holding their food in their front paws they are 'one of us'—animals with which we feel a special empathy. The flat face and large eye-patches give the giant panda a child-like appearance. Toy manufacturers are well aware of the attractions of the flatter face, and over the years the teddy-bear has undergone a slow process of evolution that has shortened the length of its muzzle. Modern teddy-bears look far more like yellow giant pandas than the grizzly bears from which they were originally modelled, although the panda might not have won such a place in human hearts were it not that the teddy-bear was already a popular toy when the first pandas began to arrive in the West. There is good evidence that a child-like face plays tricks on our brains, bypassing conscious thought and directly stirring emotions deep within the psyche. The effect is reinforced by the panda's apparently very high forehead, another baby-like feature enhanced by the conspicuous black ears.

This is an impressive list of attractions, but to become such a star, the giant panda has had to overcome a major obstacle: it is extremely rare. Up to a point rarity adds mystique and interest, but every star knows that constant exposure is necessary to prevent the fans' attention being directed elsewhere. Yet since its discovery in 1869 only 39 giant pandas have ever been permanently exported from China, and the animal has been seen in the wild by less than 50 Westerners. More people have climbed Everest. Even the great publicity machine of television has been almost impotent to help the cause, with a meagre contribution of five films of which to date only one—by *National Geographic*—has been widely screened.

1

The panda has overcome this hurdle and remained a major star because on balance it has no serious competition. Lions, chimpanzees, giraffes, bears and familiar pets like dogs, horses and cats are enormously popular, but they do not fire the public imagination in the same way. Each scrap of information about pandas is seized by a seemingly insatiable press and becomes headline news. Press conferences called by major zoos to announce a pregnancy, a birth or a death, are given coverage that might be the envy of even the most senior politicians. When Washington Zoo's female Ling Ling fell ill in 1982 she received literally thousands of 'get well' cards. With the death of the Berlin Zoo's giant panda Tian Tian, the zoo's switchboard was jammed with tearful calls offering condolences. After Lan Lan's death in Tokyo children prayed by the empty cage and, asked for his comments, the normally inscrutable Prime Minister Masayoshi Ohira's voice trembled (Anon., 1979). During her seven-year stay at Ueno Zoo she had been seen by an estimated 32 million people. On the happier occasion when Lan Lan's successor Huan Huan gave birth in 1986, 270,000 people wrote to suggest names for the cub. Another 200,000 a day called a special 'Dial-a-Panda' phone number to hear it squeal.

The red or lesser panda has received comparatively little public attention. Although it has a thick and attractive fur coat with handsome markings, it comes off badly when compared to the giant panda. Its muzzle is long and foxy (hence another of the red panda's names—the fire fox), its eyes appear much smaller, and it shares few of the giant panda's endearing habits. Although like the giant panda the red panda feeds almost exclusively on bamboo, it will occasionally catch and kill small animals and birds, which earns it another black mark in the public imagination. This lack of favour with the public is all relative of course—where red pandas are displayed in zoos they are enormously popular—but they cannot compete with the cuddly black and white bears.

In this and several other ways, the red panda has little in common with the giant panda. Although once thought to be closely related, most zoologists now believe that the two animals belong to different groups, the red panda being a specialised racoon and the giant panda a specialised bear. Were the similarities confined to their names, it would be perverse to treat the two animals in the same book, but the confusion over their relationship to each other arose in the first place because both have evolved remarkably similar adaptations to their unusual habitat. Both are bamboo eaters, and both have fore-paws specially adapted to hold their food. Their ranges overlap substantially, and within that range both species are threatened now by the same human and ecological pressures. Independent of their genetic relationship, their dependence on bamboo binds both pandas to a common destiny. If they die, they die together.

1. The First Pandas

Few wild animals have a history worth writing about. For the most part new species are 'discovered', described in the pages of some august scientific journal, and slowly become a part of our collective knowledge about the natural world. The giant panda is different in this as in so many other ways. While the story of its discovery created quite a stir in scientific circles, the subsequent capture of the first live animals and their export to Western zoos made headlines around the world, and set a puzzle that has yet to be fully solved.

First of the pandas to become known in the West was not the giant panda, however, but the red or lesser panda. Probably the first European to see one of these pretty creatures with its foxy white face and bushy tail was Nathaniel Wallich, a Danish botanist and director of the East India Company's botanical gardens in Calcutta. He sent a pelt to Major-General Thomas Hardwicke, a British army officer and amateur naturalist. The specimen was displayed to members of the Linnean Society in 1821, but neither Wallich nor Hardwicke published a full scientific description. The honour of naming the new species consequently fell by default to the French zoologist Frédéric Cuvier, who in 1825 published an account of an animal sent to him by his son-in-law, Alfred Du Vaucel, who in turn had almost certainly obtained it from Wallich.

> This animal is native to the East Indies, but we do not know to exactly which part of this region it belongs; we have been sent a skin and a general description by A. Du Vaucel. It is one of the last discoveries that he made before succumbing to the climate and his exhaustion; I propose 'Ailurus' as the generic name of the Panda, on account of its external resemblance to the cat, and for the specific name 'fulgens' because of its brilliant colours. (Cuvier, 1824–42)

It is from the red panda that both animals took their name, but how the red panda got its name in the first place, no-one really knows. Most writers give the common Nepali name as 'wah', and attribute it to the panda's 'child-like call'. Both in captivity and in the wild the animals are almost completely silent, but several early observers mention a series of short, bird-like whistles and a weak, squeaking call-note, and one report speaks of a pair making 'a most unearthly noise' at the top of a tree. In the wild red pandas are usually solitary, and whether these two were mating or fighting we are not told. When provoked, the animals make a series of cat-like spitting hisses. An adult male caught in a leg snare by a researcher at Wolong charged at his captor, jumped off the ground, and landing on all fours emitted a loud 'coughing snort' (D. G. Reid, pers. comm.). There are of course many dialects among the isolated tribesmen of the Himalayas. Brian Houghton Hodgson, veteran of the Indian civil service, pioneer student of the languages of the Himalayas, and keen amateur naturalist, recorded the panda's names in Sikkim, Nepal and Tibet—*oá, u'któnka, sakлam, thóngwáh, thó-kyé, nigálya pónya* and *yé* (Hodgson, 1847). In central Nepal the red panda is now known locally as the *hobrey* (Fleming, 1987). Of these many alternatives, only nigálya pónya even comes close to the name given by Cuvier. Unfortunately, Hodgson gave no clue as to which of the many dialects this came from, and so I have been unable to get an accurate translation. Nigálya is probably from the root *nigalo* or *ningalo* meaning cane or bamboo. The word pónya is a bit of a mystery. Other writers have assumed the phrase to mean 'bamboo eater', but there is no similar word with this meaning in any of the better-known local languages. There is, however, a Nepali word *panjā*, meaning 'the ball of the foot' or 'claw'. It would be nice to think that the phrase originally meant something like 'bamboo-footed', recognising that the red panda, like its more famous namesake, uses its unusual front paws to grasp and pull down bamboo stems. If 'panda' was a corruption of 'panjā', it would then be one of the few names that really apply equally well to either species.

Long before the giant panda borrowed its cousin's name in the West, it was of course known to the Chinese, usually as the *Bai xiong* or white bear, although many other names are known—hardly surprising in its mountainous range with many dialects and poor communications. In the Qinling mountains, it was known as the *Zhu xiong* (Wu, 1981), or bamboo bear, which suggests that in this area the local people had more than a passing knowledge of the animal's habits. Perhaps the earliest clear reference to the giant panda in Chinese literature is in a dictionary of the Qin dynasty (221–207 BC), which describes the *mo* as a white leopard with a small head, short limbs, and black and white markings which eats copper, iron and bamboo stems. The Qin rulers had their capital city not a hundred miles from panda country, and were almost certainly familiar with the giant panda. The reference to the leopard is misleading, but of course we are not dealing here with a modern concept of animal relationships. In other details the description fits the giant panda perfectly. The assertion that they eat copper and iron sounds like a complete myth, but pandas occasionally scavenge food from pots left outside peasant houses and sometimes chew up the pots afterwards. In captivity too several animals have shown that their teeth and jaws are quite capable of macerating thick aluminium bowls. This strange habit gave rise to another of the giant panda's Chinese names—*shi tie shou*, or iron-eating beast. Now it is usually known in China as the *da xiong mao* or large bear-cat, with the red panda being the *xiao xiong mao* or small bear-cat—names which suit their owners well.

In the second century AD the giant panda was a rare and semi-divine animal inside China. In the Han dynasty (206 BC–AD 24) the emperor's garden in the then capital Xian held nearly 40 rare animal species, of which the panda was the most highly treasured, and the poet Bai Juyi (AD 772–846) credited the panda with the power to prevent disease and exorcise evil spirits. Panda skins appear scattered throughut the Chinese imperial records, as gifts or tribute on great occasions of state. But the animal was totally unknown outside the secretive 'Middle Kingdom' until the declining Qing Dynasty was slowly forced to open its doors to trade and Christianity towards the end of the nineteenth century.

Christian missionaries played a central role in making Chinese wildlife known to the West, collecting plants and animals from the areas around their missions and sending them back to their native lands. On 21 March 1869 one such missionary sat writing in his room at the Catholic college of Muping. Set deep in the Min mountains, Muping was one of many semi-independent 'kingdoms' in the Tibetan borderlands, only nominally under Chinese control. The letter he was drafting to send to Paris from this isolated outpost of Christianity was to make him famous far beyond the relatively narrow scientific circle in which he had already gained a considerable reputation, but even had he realised this it is unlikely that the priest would have given it much thought.

The priest was Père Armand David. Born in the small town of Espelette on the river Nive in the Basses-Pyrénées, he spent much of his childhood collecting the insects, plants and birds' eggs of the Basque country. His father, Fructueux Dominique David, was the local doctor, justice of the peace and mayor, well placed and well qualified to encourage the boy in his studies of the local flora and fauna. Fructueux also taught his son the rudiments of medicine, in the hope that the boy would follow his own career, but Armand had different ideas. Early in life he had decided to enter the church, and at the age of 24 took his vows in the order of St Vincent de Paul and became a Lazarist priest.

The skills he learned from his father were not to be wasted. His knowledge of medicine in particular promised to be invaluable, since Père David harboured a greater ambition: to become a missionary in China. Two years after his ordination in 1850 he wrote to his superior: 'I never stop dreaming at night about joining the Chinese Mission. For the past twelve years I have thought of nothing else than working for the salvation of non-believers.' (Quoted in de Havilland, 1987:21.)

Nothing came of the letter, and others like it, for almost ten years, but eventually the determined and tireless young priest got his way. He was summoned to Paris where he met with a Monseigneur Mouly and two other priests. These four were to be the staff of a small school in Beijing,[1] where Père David was to teach science to about a hundred boys. His reputation as a naturalist preceded him, and before leaving Paris Monseigneur Mouly introduced him to Henri Milne-Edwards, director of the Muséum d'Histoire Naturelle. Milne-Edwards asked David if he would collect specimens of any interesting plants and animals he happened to find, a commission to which the priest happily agreed, no doubt thinking this would make an interesting diversion from his main work as a missionary and teacher.

It cannot have taken David very long to realise that the task of converting the Chinese to Christianity was going to be long and difficult. A letter to his godfather reads: 'Above all do not think China will become Catholic. At the pace things are going now, it will take forty or fifty thousand years before the whole Empire is converted' (Quoted in Fox, 1949:xvi). Perhaps this helped him to accept the instructions of his superiors that his missionary work should take second place to his collecting. The material he sent back to France soon after his arrival in China was well chosen and well prepared, and the staff at the natural history museum were impressed. Henri Milne-Edwards quickly used his considerable influence to persuade the Superior General of the Lazarist order that this gifted missionary should undertake more work for the museum, sponsored by the French government. By the spring of 1866 Père David was leaving Beijing for Mongolia, entrusted with the task of collecting as much of the wildlife of the area as he could.

During his twelve years in China David discovered some 58 species of bird, about a hundred new insects, many snails and several fish. (There would have been more fish, but the Chinese alcohol he used to preserve them on their journey back to France was too weak for the task!) Many of the plants he collected are now common in the gardens of Europe and North America but were then unknown in the West. Some of these discoveries are named after the priest. There is the early spring-flowering peach *Prunus davidiana*, with its delicate pink blossoms; the lily *Lilium davidi*, standing an imposing six-feet tall and topped with a profusion of orange-red flowers; the butterfly bush, *Buddleia davidi*, with its purple sprays; and *Clematis davidi*, a shrubby climber with clusters of small, slate-blue flowers. Slightly less well known is the dove tree, *Davidia involucrata*, a relict of the ice age and already rare in David's time.

Despite the importance of this vast collection, there is no doubt that Père David is now best remembered for his mammal finds. By a strange quirk of fate, few of these now bear his name, the one notable exception being the animal he called the milou, *Elaphurus davidiensis*, now known in English as Père David's deer. This strange beast with its peculiar splayed hooves had already been extinct in the wild for 1,700 years when David arrived in China, but a captive population had been maintained in the Imperial Park in Beijing. During his first stay in that city David obtained two skins of the deer, probably as a result of devious dealings with the guards at the Imperial Park. This cannot have been easy, since the sentence for anyone killing the animals was death. Shortly afterwards the French Legation persuaded the superintendent of the imperial estates to allow three live animals to be exported to Europe. Sadly, none of these survived the journey, and it is very fortunate that other animals followed because in 1894 a flood undermined the walls of the Imperial Park, allowing the animals to escape. Very few survived the attentions of the starving people of Beijing, and almost all those that did were slaughtered by Imperial troops in 1900.

Another remarkable mammal find was the golden monkey, a creature of staggering beauty and agility still little known outside China. The scientific name *Rhinopithecus roxellanae* credits not its discoverer but the mistress of Sultan Suleiman II, Roxellane. The pert, turned-up nose and ginger hair apparently reminded Alphonse Milne-Edwards of a portrait of the famous courtesan when he came to name the species.

Alphonse Milne-Edwards was Henri's son, and it was to him that Père David wrote from his room in the Catholic College of Muping. Humble and almost apologetic, he began by listing his latest acquisitions—a goral, two cats, and a takin. In the previous month it seems he had found only six or eight species that might eventually turn out to be new to science, and obviously felt this to be a poor return for his efforts. Then, almost as a footnote he added:

> As my collection will not arrive in Paris for some time, I would ask you to publish quickly the following brief description of a bear which appears to be new to science.
> Ursus melanoleucus A.D.
> Very large according to my hunters.

Ears short.

Hair fairly short; beneath the four feet very hairy.

Colours: white, with the ears, the surroundings of the eyes, the tip of the tail and the four legs brownish black. The black on the forelegs is joined over the back in a straight band. I have just received a young bear of this kind and have seen the mutilated skins of adult specimens. The colours are always the same and equally distributed. I have not seen this species, which is easily the prettiest kind of animal I know, in the museums of Europe; perhaps it is new to science! (Milne-Edwards, 1869).

The animal was of course a giant panda. Two days later his hunters bought Père David a freshly killed young panda, and his diary records the occasion with characteristically dispassionate accuracy.

My Christian hunters return today after a ten-day absence. They bring me a young white bear, which they took alive but unfortunately killed so that it could be carried more easily. . . . The young white bear, which they sell me very dearly,[2] is all white except for the legs, ears and around the eyes which are deep black. The colours are the same as those I saw in the skin of an adult bear the other day at the home of Li, the hunter. This must be a new species of Ursus, very remarkable because of its colour, but also for its paws, which are hairy underneath, and for other characters. (David, 1874)

It was at the home of 'Li the hunter' that Père David had first seen a giant panda skin. Returning on 11 March 1869 from a long day's walk, he was invited to rest at the home of the principal landowner of the valley, who served him and his Chinese assistant with tea and sweets.

At this heathen's house I see a skin of the famous black and white bear, which appears to be very large. It is a remarkable species, and I am delighted when my hunters tell me that I shall certainly soon procure this animal; tomorrow, they tell me, they will go out to kill this carnivore (sic) which should make an interesting novelty for science.

In fact, his hunters provided David with two giant panda specimens, for on 1 April they produced the carcass of an adult female.

They bring me a white bear which they tell me is fully adult. Its colours are exactly like those of the young one I have, only the darker parts are less black and the white more soiled. The animal's head is very big, and the snout round and short instead of being pointed as it is in the Asian black bear.

The experienced and meticulous Père David was certainly aware that his new acquisitions were peculiar. In his description to Milne-Edwards he noted the hairy paws and can hardly have missed the false thumb, though he makes no mention of it in this report. It must also have been at about this time that he obtained the description of the animal's peculiar diet from his hunters, which he included in the notes he published on his return to France.

Another interesting new animal which I have seen in the mountains is the black and white bear, although some of the skeletal characters distance it from the true bears and relate it to the pandas: M. Milne-Edwards has created for this animal the genus *Ailuropus*. This animal, which the hunters call Paé-shioung (white bear), is much rarer than the black or Tibetan bear which lives in the same forests;

It also lives at higher altitude and appears to have a vegetable diet. But nevertheless, it is said that it does not refuse meat when the chance presents itself, and I even think this may be its principal food in winter, when it does not hibernate. Moreover, the lesser panda, *Ailurus fulgens*, which is also common in these woods, supplements its diet with meat, which ordinarily consists of vegetables, fruits, leaves, buds, and wild bamboo shoots according to the season. (David, 1871)

Père David was already familiar with the red panda from Cuvier's description, and only two days after obtaining his second giant panda at Muping, his hunters bought him a specimen.

As regards mammals, I got a young wild boar striped like the European, a Chantché-oua or panda and a rock antelope. The panda is an interesting animal already known in the Himalayas and formerly abundant in these forests but now scarce. My hunters tell me that this plantigrade animal lives in trees and in holes, and that its food is vegetable or animal according to the occasion. The Chinese call it 'child of the mountain' because its voice imitates that of a child.

Next day, a second red panda arrived, and Père David noted in his diary that 'Its paws and head resemble those of my white bear.' There is no doubt then that Père David noticed the similarities between the two animals but with his limited resources in the college at Muping he was in no position to carry out the detailed anatomical work necessary to establish a solid connection. In the circumstances the choice of scientific name was obvious. Externally, the giant panda so closely resembles a bear that any other name would have been foolish.

The opportunity to dissect the carcasses and the honour of giving the giant panda its accepted scientific name thus fell to Alphonse Milne-Edwards in Paris, who in 1870 published a brief note about the discovery.

Without doubt the most interesting animal is that which M. l'Abbé David has referred to under the name of *Ursus melanoleuca*. In its external form it much resembles a bear, but skeletal and dental characters distinguish it from bears and relate it to the pandas and raccoons. It thus constitutes a new genus, which I have called *Ailuropoda*. (Milne-Edwards, 1870)

In a later and detailed description of the panda, Milne-Edwards changed the name to *Ailuropus* (panda-like) 'to recall the resemblance between the feet of this animal and those of the (red) panda'. He believed that under the rules of taxonomic naming the name *Ailuropoda* was not valid because it had already been used in another context—in Gray's *Catalogue of Carnivorous, Pachydermatous and Edentate Mammalia in the British Museum*. This created general confusion, compounded by Flower and Lydekker in *Mammals Living and Extinct* who decided to correct the Latin spelling and changed both names—to *Aelurus* for the red and *Aeluropus* for the giant panda. For a considerable time all three names for the giant panda were in use in the scientific literature. At the same time the dispute in scientific circles over the relationship of the panda even managed to confuse its common name. In France both animals had always been known as pandas, but in England the giant panda was known as the parti-coloured bear until 1901. Its name was changed as the result of a recommendation by the director of the British Museum of Natural History, E. Ray Lankester. Shortly after taking up his post in 1898 he had examined the museum's collection of bones, and concluded from these that the giant panda was more closely related to the red panda than to the bears and suggested that it should be known as the 'great panda' (Lankester, 1901).

Père Armand David was never to see a giant panda in the wild. His final journey to China took him to the Shaanxi and Gansu, where he spent some three months collecting in the Qinling mountains. These mountains were, and still are, home to a sizable population of giant pandas, but there is no mention at all of the panda in his journals for this period (David, 1875). Finally, prostrated by fever, he returned to France in 1874. His position as a priest prevented him from receiving all the recognition to which his pioneering work had entitled him, but following his recovery from illness he spent a happy and contented life working mainly on his vast collection until his death in 1900.

For almost half a century little more was heard of the giant panda. A few skins and skeletons purchased from local hunters by missionaries or diplomatic staff of foreign embassies in China made their way into European museums. Occasional notes were published on the panda's habits in the wild, gleaned from local people or from a study of the animal's tracks. But it was becoming obvious that the giant panda was in fact a rarity.

Possibly the first Westerner to actually see a giant panda in the wild was one J. Houston Edgar, a romantic, poet, explorer and missionary under the China Inland Mission in the Tibetan borderlands. In 1924 he wrote a letter to the *China Journal* recording a strange sighting in wild country along the upper reaches of the River Yangtze.

> In 1916, when about half way between Batang and Derge, and in wild country not far from the Kin Sha, I saw an animal asleep in the forks of a high oak tree which has puzzled me ever since. It was very large, seemed quite white, and was curled up in a great ball very much after the manner of cats. It was unknown, and a source of wonder, to my Tibetans.

Although this may have been a panda, the location given is some 200 km west of the presently known range. A similar, doubtful sighting was reported by Brigadier-General G. E. Pereira, who travelled western China and eastern Tibet hoping to shoot a panda, but it is quite possible that no Westerner set eyes on a live panda until 1914 when the German zoologist Hugo Weigold was presented with a live cub by local hunters. The cub was still suckling, and since Weigold was unable to provide it with suitable food, it soon died. Its skin, along with five others purchased from local hunters, eventually went on display in the Berlin Museum (Sowerby, 1937).

In the 1920s much of the eastern edge of the Tibetan plateau was still marked on Western maps as 'unknown', with rivers and mountain ranges pencilled in with dotted lines that marked their presumed course. The romance of exploration, and the possibility of being the first Westerners to shoot a giant panda had an irresistible appeal for many big-game hunters. The honour—if it can be so called—fell to Kermit and Theodore Roosevelt,

Figure 1. Routes taken by Père David and by Theodore and Kermit Roosevelt to reach the mountains of western Sichuan.

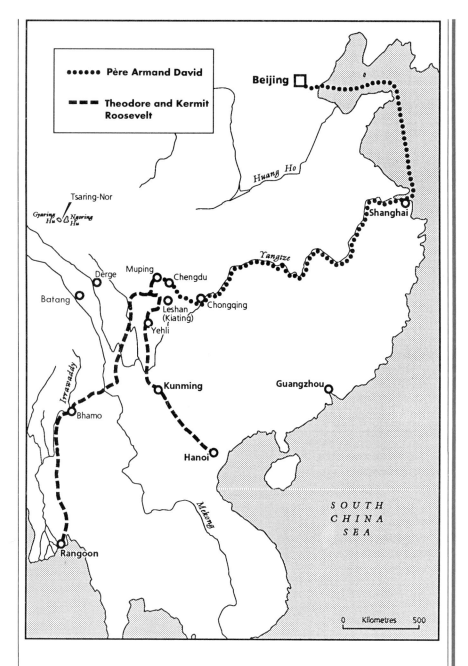

whose father, President Theodore Roosevelt, had given his sons a yearning for adventure. Their political connections proved essential to the success of the trip, for it was only after the intervention of the State Department that the Chinese government could be persuaded to allow the foreigners to enter their borderlands. Eventually, with funds from William V. Kelly, a patron of the Field Museum of Chicago, the brothers left New York in November 1928 to sail for Burma. Travelling from Rangoon by train to

Kathá, and by river-steamer along the Irrawaddy river, they reached Bhamo on Christmas Eve and headed north with a team of 30 mules along the old trade route from Burma into China. After three months hard walking through the mountains of Yunnan and Sichuan they arrived in Muping, where with 14 native hunters they spent six days searching the forests 'without seeing a wild animal of any sort'. They had given up all hope of even seeing a giant panda in the wild when a week later and a hundred miles to the south they were told of a panda that had raided a beehive a month previously. Three further days hunting again produced no sight of a panda. Then, while hunting takin near Yehli on 23 April, the hunters stumbled across giant panda tracks in the snow. Though the tracks were evidently old, they followed them for two and a half hours, but were once again on the verge of giving up when one of the guides spotted the animal dozing in a large hollow tree. A moment later it was dead, killed by simultaneous shots from both brothers.

The Roosevelts' shooting of a giant panda set off an avalanche of Western hunting expeditions, often sponsored by museums eager for specimens to grace their exhibition halls. In 1931 the Philadelphia Academy of Natural Sciences sent a large expedition, headed by Brooke Dolan. This group obtained three adult specimens from local hunters, and a fourth shot by a member of the expedition, Ernst Schaefer, a young German naturalist. They were followed in 1934 by the Sage West China expedition, sponsored by the American Museum of Natural History, which accounted for the third panda to be killed by Westerners. Almost at the end of their time in China, Dean Sage and William Sheldon decided to have one final attempt at hunting pandas before returning home. After walking for most of the day, their dogs disturbed a panda which fortuitously headed straight towards them. Their account of what happened next (Sage, 1935) well portrays the excitement these early hunters felt.

All of a sudden I heard the unmistakable noise of breaking bamboos, and the barking became louder. Wong said, 'Beishung!'
  Even at this moment, it did not occur to me that we should ever see the animal. If indeed the dogs had started one out, the chances were he would go crashing off into the bamboos and that would be the end of it. Nevertheless, I took my gun and tried to put a cartridge in the chamber. It was all covered with snow and ice from the recent hard going, and the shell would not go in, so I threw it away—an act which was later to become of the utmost importance—and put in another one. Above me, Bill began to climb to gain a better vantage point, but I was in an ideal spot and did not move. Up the ravine came the dogs, their barking growing steadily louder, and the bamboos crackling at a great rate. Suddenly, I heard the deep, angry growl of a large animal, and I began to get really excited. And then—as if in a dream—I saw a giant panda coming through the bamboos about sixty yards away from me. He was heading straight up the ravine with the dogs at his heels. I fired but missed. The panda made a right angle turn and came straight for the ledge I was standing on. I fired again.
  He came right on, not running—walking rapidly is the only way to describe it. His head hung low and swayed from side to side. His tongue was out, and he was panting. He appeared to be looking at the ground, and apparently did not see me at all. I frantically worked the bolt of my rifle and snapped the hammer on an

empty chamber. In a daze, thoughts flashed through my mind: 'No more bullets; what'll I do? He's only twenty feet away, now fifteen, he's coming straight at me. Can I kill him with the butt of my rifle?' I felt a cartridge thrust in my hand. Wong had seen my predicament and picked up the one I had discarded. I jammed it in the gun and fired into the beishung's fur. He was less than ten feet from me! At the same moment Bill shot from above, and the animal, struck simultaneously by both our bullets, rolled over and over down the slope and came to stop against a tree fifty yards below.

We had killed a giant panda.

Other skins and carcasses followed to the West, usually bought from local hunters by missionaries or Western expeditions. Only one further panda was shot by a Westerner, a Briton by the name of Captain Courtney Brocklehurst, but the enthusiasm was dwindling. By 1936 the great challenge was no longer to shoot a panda, but to capture one and ship it back to a Western zoo alive.

At this point the story begins to read like the script for a soap opera. Initially, there were two main characters, both rich, both colourful and both American, at least by birth. The plot was set in motion by William Harvest Harkness Jr, son of a New York City lawyer, and Harvard graduate with a hankering for exotic travel and adventure. In 1934 he had collected several Komodo dragons in the Dutch East Indies and delivered them to the Bronx Zoo in New York, and by the summer of that year he was making preparations to provide the zoo with a live giant panda. In the spirit of the times, the trip was also to include a study of ancient stone inscriptions in Peru, a visit to the Solomon Islands to photograph hill tribes, and a talk with descendants of pirate chiefs in the Philippines (Anon., 1934). His last-minute marriage to his long-time friend Ruth McCombs was not allowed to interfere with his plans. She wanted to join him on the trip, but was persuaded that a lone woman on an expedition with five men might create friction. Two weeks later, on 22 September 1934, he sailed from New York, never to see her again.

When the expedition finally arrived in Shanghai in January 1935, things began to go badly wrong. After several months of frustrated attempts to gain the necessary permits for his expedition, formal permission from the Academia Sinica in Nanking was refused. William Harkness was devastated. He took a train from Nanking to Shanghai, and nothing was heard of him for two weeks. Eventually he was tracked down by a US marshal to a Shanghai hotel where he had registered under an assumed name. Taken before the District Attorney of the US court in Shanghai to account for his disappearance, Harkness explained that he had merely been trying to 'forget' his bitter disappointment at his failure to obtain a permit, and that he intended to leave soon for home (*New York Times*, 5 Apr. 1935).

Harkness's fortunes were about to change however, at least temporarily. Soon after his brush with the law he met up with the veteran hunter Floyd Tangier Smith,[3] the second and without doubt the more experienced of the two actors in the plot. Born in Yokohama in 1882 of American missionary parents, Tangier Smith returned to America in 1900 and attended the Kenyon Military Academy in Ohio before moving on to the New England colleges of Dartmouth and Bowdoin. After his graduation in 1908 he joined the International Banking Corporation. His position guaranteed him a comfortable life, but he seems to have become disenchanted with his work and in 1914 he joined the American Trading Company, based at first in New York and later in India and Shanghai. Here he eventually quit his job to become a full-time hunter. From 1930 to 1932 he had worked in Sichuan, leading the Marshall Field Zoological Expedition to South East Asia, and was an official collector for the Field Museum of Natural History in Chicago. His skill in looking after the animals he collected and in taxi-dermy soon won him respect, and his contacts within the Chinese government and institutions were excellent. His biggest difficulties were no doubt the practical ones of working in western Sichuan. Although nominally under Chinese rule, the country had been depopulated by bandits and disease, and was one of the few areas in China where people were so poor that some adult women went naked. In addition, troops loyal to Chiang Kai Shek were roaming the mountains in search of the Red Army soldiers led by Mao Zedong. In this generally unfriendly climate anything could happen, and often did. On one occasion Tangier Smith's camp was burned to the ground, and his equipment and many of his specimens destroyed. The expedition members were working away from the camp at the time, and injury and death were averted 'rather as a result of sheer good luck and a policy of keeping out of trouble than as a result of any special prowess on our part' (*New York Times*, 29 Dec. 1932).

According to contemporary reports, Harkness and Smith were in Sichuan together by July 1935, along with a young Englishman, Gerald Russell, who had recently graduated from Cambridge and gone to Shanghai in search of adventure. The party had only been a few days in Kiating when a telegram arrived from the US Consul in Hankow instructing Smith and Harkness to return to the east because of a breach of passport regulations. Being British, Russell was exempt and remained in Sichuan until the end of the summer (*North China Daily News*, 31 July 1935).

The two men returned to Shanghai, hoping to get back into the mountains of Sichuan before the winter made roads impassable. Tangier Smith's main interest at this point was to take photographs and make field studies of takin—grotesque goat-antelopes related to musk oxen—which were to be used in the construction of an exhibit in the Field Museum (*China Press*, 9 Oct. 1935). He was also interested in pandas, of course, but expected no more than to obtain a complete carcass. It was Harkness who determined to bring a panda back alive.

Sadly, William Harkness was not destined to fulfil his dream. Exactly how and when he returned to the city we do not know, but by February 1936 he lay dead in a Shanghai sanatorium. Several causes for his death have been reported—viral fever, Hodgkin's disease, and lead poisoning as a result of treatment for syphilis being the commonest. The truth seems to be that he died after three operations in an attempt to remove a tumour of the throat, an illness which he had kept hidden even from his wife.

At this point the third player enters the plot. Ruth McCombs, now Ruth Harkness, was in her own words 'a New York dress designer with a distaste for all exercise and a strong inclination to get about only in taxis' (*New York Times*, 20 Feb. 1936). Diminutive and elegant, she did not know how to fire a gun, and was not interested in learning. As she wrote later,

> I wouldn't have known a tragopan pheasant from a tufted deer, but I felt pretty certain there would be no mistaking a panda, if I ever saw one. I had seen pictures of the mounted specimens that a museum had, and certainly it never could be confused with any other animal in the world. The markings are unmistakable. (Harkness, 1938)

On hearing of her husband's death she decided to take up the reins of his expedition—encouraged by Gerald Russell, who had returned to New York and pointed out to Ruth that by doing so she could fulfil her husband's wish and put to use the mass of equipment scattered between Shanghai and Chengdu. In view of her credentials it is hardly surprising that her decision met with solicitous warnings from her friends and ridicule from everyone else. She was unperturbed. As she recorded later in her book *The Lady and the Panda*:

> in spite of what my friends and family had to say, I decided that it was up to me to do what I could in the way of carrying on. Everything was there in China for me to work with; it was an opportunity, an excuse for adventure that would probably never come again. I had wanted to go in the first place, so why not now?

She wrote to Tangier Smith and asked him to help her carry on the hunt, and two months later she was aboard the liner *Tancred*, bound for China.

Arriving in Shanghai, she checked into the Palace Hotel where her husband had stayed after his disappointment in Nanking. The first week she spent visiting the American consulate to settle her late husband's affairs, and talking to a character who she refers to in her book as 'Zoology' Jones, one of William Harkness's associates on his last ill-fated attempt to reach panda country.

There can be no doubt that this 'Zoology' Jones was in fact Tangier Smith, and it is rare in untangling this complex tale to find anything certain. Her description fits him perfectly. His age and his hunting experience are right, and the 'stories of racehorses he had owned' that he told her were probably by way of explaining his nickname 'Ajax', the name of his favourite mount. Furthermore, there is the evidence of the German animal dealer Otto Focklemann, who in 1964 clearly remembered being told by Tangier Smith that Ruth Harkness had visited him in hospital many times (Fockelmann, 1964).

Like everyone else, Tangier Smith told Ruth Harkness that she had little hope of catching a panda, and suggested that she go along with him on his next trip and settle for bringing back less exotic game. She declined the offer and their association was amicably terminated (*North China Daily News*, 6 Dec. 1936). Soon afterwards she flew to Beijing where she met with more patronising ridicule from the American consul, and a dose of bronchitis.

The illness delayed her plans, which proved to be a stroke of luck. As she was recovering she received a call from the American-born Chinese hunter Jack Young. Young had been with the successful Roosevelt expedition and had provided panda specimens for the Shanghai museum. He was unable to accompany her himself but offered the services of his younger brother Quentin. Well educated and a fluent speaker of English, Cantonese and the Sichuan dialect of Mandarin, Quentin was a keen hunter who had already been on several trips with his elder brother including three to Sichuan to collect animals for museums in China and America (Sowerby, 1936).

Quentin was duly taken on as expedition leader, and soon showed himself to be a proficient organiser. On 26 September the modestly equipped expedition left Shanghai to begin the 1,500 mile journey up the Yangtze River to Chongqing. Then travelling by car to Chengdu, and on foot to Wenchuan (with an uninvited escort of Nationalist soldiers) they reached the edge of panda country. Sitting in the loft of a buddhist temple in Wenchuan, they met the man who was to be their guide.

> Wild grey hair escaping from a dirty white turban carelessly slipping over one ear, an ancient skin coat with the fur inside, something made of leather that was half boots and half gaiters and held up to his waist by strings, and over it all a loose, homespun garment bunched up around him with a rope. He tethered two mongrel dogs with tinkling bells to the foot of the ladder, and mumbling to himself mounted to the loft.

This was Lao Tsang, a headman of the district and a hunter, who lived in the mountains. He knew where pandas could be found, and although he disliked foreigners, he was prepared to make an exception in the case of Ruth Harkness.

Lao Tsang was hired, and the expedition left the next day, turning west into the Qionglai mountains from Wenchuan, and into the area that is now the Wolong Reserve but was then part of the semi-autonomous 'Kingdom of Wassu'. After several days hard climbing, they set up camp near the village of Tsaopo where Quentin set about finding native hunters and scouting the surrounding countryside. Within a few days a network of trapping camps had been set up, and Ruth Harkness moved higher into the valley, to settle in the base camp for what she expected to be a long wait. But she was quickly irritated by some of her companions, especially the wife of one of the hunters whose endless hacking and spitting in her tent 'wore her nerves ragged'. So she eagerly accepted the suggestion that she should go to stay for a few days in Quentin's camp and learn something about trapping.

The lesson was to be a brief one. The party set off the next morning. They had examined only a single trap and were pushing through thick bamboo towards a second when a shout went up from the path ahead.

> I heard Lao Tsang yell, the report of his blunderbuss musket, and then Quentin's voice raised in rapid and imperious Chinese. Falling, stumbling or being dragged by Yang, we crashed through the bamboo. I caught a glimpse of Quentin through the almost impenetrable wet green wall, and got close enough to gasp, 'What is it?'
> 'Bei shung', was the terse reply.

Despite strict orders to the contrary, Lao Tsang had fired at a panda and missed. Then, as they moved on again, Quentin suddenly stopped short.

He listened intently for a split second, and then went ploughing on so rapidly I couldn't keep up with him. Dimly through the waving wet branches I saw him near a huge rotting tree. I stumbled on blindly, brushing the water from my face and eyes. Then I too stopped, frozen in my tracks. From the dead old tree came a baby's whimper.

I must have been momentarily paralysed for I didn't move until Quentin came toward me and held out his arms. There in the palms of his two hands was a squirming baby Bei shung.

The cub was rushed back to Kwanhsien, fed *en route* on dried powdered milk from a Chinese nursing-bottle, both of which Ruth Harkness had taken with her. From there she was taken once again by car to Chengdu, and by plane to Shanghai. Then began 16 days of total chaos, the visits of friends and well-wishers having to be squeezed into a 24-hour feeding schedule. Ruth Harkness and the panda now called Su Lin after Jack Young's wife, successfully avoided most of the local press for a while, giving interviews only the day before she was due to sail for America. But word leaked out, and she was apprehended at the docks and her passage delayed for five days. Eventually, despite having 'organised a scientific expedition' without the proper authority, and attempting to take the animal out of the country without a proper permit, the Chinese customs were persuaded to allow her and her precious cargo to leave. On 2 December Ruth Harkness and Su Lin boarded the *President McKinley*, Ruth Harkness clutching an export permit and a ticket for Su Lin—One Dog, $20.00 Shanghai. Sixteen days later, 'Dog' and owner arrived safely in San Francisco.

The story was a journalist's dream. The rarest large mammal in the world had been captured in the remote mountains of war-torn China and brought back alive to the West; not by some rude brute of a hunter, but by an attractive and sophisticated woman. As if this were not enough in itself, the animal was no ferocious killer but a blotched bundle of fur that chewed endearingly at her sleeve as she held it for the photographers. In a few brief moments on the dockside, one animal did more for the cause of nature conservation than most humans could hope to achieve in a lifetime.

Ruth Harkness and Su Lin became world famous almost overnight. Su Lin was visited by the Roosevelts, Brooke Dolan, and Dean Sage; Ruth Harkness became the first woman to speak at the annual banquet of the New York Explorer's Club.

Back in Shanghai Tangier Smith was saddened and frustrated. He asserted that his hunters had located the mother panda three months previously, and had watched her 'build her nest'. They knew that the baby panda had been born, and were only waiting until it was weaned before attempting to capture both mother and baby together (*New York Times*, 4 Dec. 1936). At first he was inclined to believe that Ruth Harkness had been entirely innocent of any intentional misconduct and that she had not been aware of the circumstances surrounding her find. Early in December 1936 he gave an interview to the *China Press* in order to 'make it clear that he was not charging Mrs. Harkness with having made away with or in any sense stolen a panda belonging to him in the course of her capture of the only live panda in captivity' (*China Press*, 11 Dec. 1936; see also Smith, E., 1936).

By July 1937 Tangier Smith was less sympathetic, angered in part by rumours circulating in Shanghai that before her departure Ruth Harkness had been slandering his good name. During a recent trip to Sichuan he had also discovered that the panda had actually been sold to her by one of his own hunters, a man he names as Koo (*Shanghai Evening Post and Mercury*, 24 July 1937). This version of events was much later confirmed by a letter from Gerald Russell to Richard Reynolds, an Atlanta lawyer who during the 1960s took great pains to try to uncover the truth of this story. In this letter Russell asserts that when the party had spent ten days in camp, Su Lin was bought from a local hunter for $60 Shanghai (Russell, 1965). Another version of the story is similar, although it contradicts Gerald Russell's account in important details. According to Leslie Kilborn, a physiologist working at the West China Union University, Ruth Harkness bought the animal from some men who she met in a tea-shop in Kwanhsien who happened to be playing with a cub they had secured for Tangier Smith and were taking to Chengdu (Kilborn, 1965).

As increasingly vitriolic accusations began to fly in the press, Tangier Smith categorically called Ruth Harkness a liar and challenged her to sue for libel, but he really did not have much enthusiasm for sensationalism and in an interview given to the BBC radio programme 'The World Goes By' in October 1937 he was more typically restrained.

> It has been my great good fortune to have been the active agent in effecting the capture of the only three giant pandas that have ever been taken alive. That has been possible only after some several years of careful study of the animal's habits and the systematic organization of the inhabitants in a certain area. My central collecting headquarters are at a village called Chaopo[4] . . . The first specimen thus secured—the baby panda recently sold to Chicago—it was not my privilege to take home myself. It had been brought into Chaopo at a time when I was absent some several days before a party of travellers pitched their camp about fifteen miles up the valley from Chaopo, and it was sold to them for a tempting cash price. There were more than forty animals and birds collected in the camp at the same time, but nothing but the panda was purchased by the visitors, and I brought most of the others with me on this trip to England.

It is still impossible to be absolutely certain of what happened. Ruth Harkness's own account is consistent throughout her interviews with the press and in her book. True, she is deceptive in her description of Tangier Smith, but by the time she came to write her book, he was already angry over her 'theft' of his panda, and so it is perhaps hardly surprising that she gives him a pseudonym. If this is the limit of her ability to deceive then she was a poor liar, for her description of 'Zoology' Jones is transparent. According to Smith, she made a promise not to encroach on his territory around Tsaopo (*New York Times*, 4 Dec. 1936), but even he himself agrees that she might not have realised where she was being taken. Fabulous though it is, her story rings true.

Perhaps there is another explanation. According to Ruth Harkness, all finances had been put in the hands of Quentin Young, to the extent that when she finally returned to Shanghai she had only sacrificial paper money in her purse. Quentin thus had the means to buy information, and in Lao

Tsang perhaps found a willing accomplice. Lao Tsang did not like foreigners and refused to work for them, we are told. Why not? What foreigners might he, a hunter in the wilds of Sichuan, have met in the past? Apart from Tangier Smith, hardly anyone else had been there. And why agree to work for Ruth Harkness?

Could it be that Lao Tsang had a grudge against Tangier Smith? This would not be surprising, since Smith had little regard for the local people, and probably found his distaste hard to disguise. In an article for *Home and Empire* he later wrote

> It was a long job teaching these hunters that there is a difference between a live animal and a dead one, and getting them to treat their captures carefully so as not to injure them, for they are primitive, stupid, and deceitful, and they lie with the greatest of ease. (Smith, 1937)

Perhaps Lao Tsang already knew that Tangier Smith's hunters were keeping an eye on the cub. As a Chinese speaker and Chinese national Quentin Young would have understood that beneath the rags of this 'ignorant peasant' lived a human being quite clever enough to see a way of avenging some past wrong. Using either his natural charm or the money he had been given by Ruth Harkness, it would not be difficult for Quentin to persuade Lao Tsang to tell him where the maternity den was located. They could then lead Ruth Harkness right to the spot, so that she would be there when the baby panda was 'discovered'. The only difficulty would be the cub's mother, which was almost certain to attack anyone venturing too close to the maternity den. This would explain why when Lao Tsang 'suddenly caught a glimpse of a full-grown panda drifting silently as smoke into the jungle ahead of him he forgot completely the strict orders he had been given and fired'.

Quentin Young is still living, now happily settled in America, and not surprisingly he denies this version of events. His own story agrees in every detail with that of Ruth Harkness. He claims that with the help of local hunters he learned the signs to look for, but far from being thrilled with the discovery of the baby, his pride was wounded when he found that Ruth Harkness was 'satisfied with this infant creature and prepared for it with baby goods.' He attributes their success to good luck and to his ability to speak Chinese and so quickly gain the confidence of the local people. As a foreigner who knew little Chinese, Tangier Smith was 'fair game' for the locals, according to Young—and as a foreigner who has tried to work in the area I must agree that this also has a ring of truth about it. Tangier Smith thought pandas would be difficult to capture and 'the Chinese in typical fashion allowed him to think so' (Young, 1983). Another reason to doubt that Su Lin had first been captured and kept by native hunters is that when discovered by Ruth Harkness the cub was little more than a month old, which we know with some certainty since its first tooth erupted on the day of its arrival in San Francisco. Tangier Smith is repeatedly critical of the hunters' inability to keep even the most adaptable animals alive, and even allowing for his prejudice it seems unlikely that the hunters could have kept a young panda alive for more than a day or two at most. It is doubtful if the real truth of these conflicting accounts will ever be known.

According to Ruth Harkness, the expedition, not including the money spent by her husband, had cost $20,000, but no zoo was prepared to pay this sort of money for even the most exotic of all animals. After much haggling Su Lin eventually found a home at the Brookfield Zoo in Chicago. Ruth Harkness received $14,000 which she used to finance a return trip to China, the object being to acquire a mate for Su Lin.

August 1937 saw Ruth Harkness back in Shanghai, but in the previous six months there had been great changes in China. For six years the Japanese invasion of China had met with little resistance, Chiang Kai Shek being more interested in defeating the Communists than the Japanese army. However, following negotiations in July 1937, Communists and Nationalists joined forces and the war escalated dramatically. On 11 August Japanese marines landed at Shanghai docks, and on 13 August there was savage fighting in the city. Two days after Ruth Harkness first checked in to the Palace Hotel the building was bombed by the Japanese, and it quickly became clear that she stood no chance of repeating her former journey up the Yangtze. On 21 August she left Shanghai once again, bound this time for Hanoi with the intention of entering west China through Yunnan (Anon., 1937a). Eventually she reached Tsaopo, where she spent three months organising local hunters. Male cubs were not to be found, but on 18 December 1937 hunters in the Samulin mountains captured two females, a subadult and a 2.7-kg cub. The subadult would eat only bamboo and died before reaching Chengdu (Anon., 1938a), but the cub slowly recovered from its long journey across the mountains. She was quickly flown from Chengdu to Shanghai, where an impromptu exhibition in the bar of the Shanghai Club raised $700 for the Shanghai Children's Refugee Hospital (Anon., 1938b).

At first the new panda was named Diana, after Quentin Young's wife, but soon after her arrival in America she picked up the Chinese nickname of Mei Mei. Mei Mei promised to be a companion, if not a mate for Su Lin. Then, on April Fools' Day 1938 Su Lin died suddenly. The post mortem failed to establish the cause of death, although it dismissed an early suggestion that she might have succumbed to an infection of the throat after scratching herself while trying to eat oak twigs. But it did at last correctly establish her sex—male. In 1938 Ruth Harkness returned to China for a third time, in order to try to obtain a mate for Mei Mei. She had been planning the trip for some months when a cable arrived from Quentin Young to tell her that he had captured a live male. Immediately she changed her plans, flying to Chengdu via San Francisco and Hong Kong in less than eight days, where she found Quentin with an adult male and a young female. But for the first time things went badly wrong. The male went berserk during a thunderstorm. He broke out of his cage and became extremely savage and eventually had to be shot. The female too was a difficult, intractable creature. Rather than take it to America she decided to release it back into the wild.

The Bronx Zoo had refused to buy Su Lin from Ruth Harkness in 1936, but the publicity she brought to Chicago's Brookfield Zoo had made all American zoos aware of her value. The Bronx needed a panda, and in

March 1938 Dean Sage, himself a one-time panda-hunter and now a trustee of the New York Zoological Society, began making enquiries of his contacts at the West China Union University. He wrote to Dr Frank Dickinson (whose garden incidentally housed some of Tangier Smith's animal collection) suggesting that the zoo would provide research materials for the university in exchange for their help in collecting animals for the zoo. Within two months a young female was on her way to New York. In an editorial the *New York Times* ventured to 'put in a word for the large American minority that is getting rather tired of the giant panda' (*New York Times*, 8 June 1938), but three days later Pandora's picture was inevitably on their back page.

Meanwhile, back in China Tangier Smith had not been idle. In June 1937 hunters working for him had succeeded in trapping not one but two adult pandas, one a 90-kg male, the other a 45-kg female (*New York Times*, 3 July 1937). The male died only a week after he was captured, from blood poisoning which developed as a result of an injury to the animal's foot when it was trapped, but the female, named Jennie (Sowerby, 1938), was dyed brown in order not to attract attention on her journey out of the country (*The Times*, 24 July 1937). Smith was at pains to make it clear that this was not to deceive the authorities, from whom he had all the necessary permissions, but to protect the animal from the unwelcome attention of crowds. Jennie sailed on board the liner *André Lebon* on 25 July 1937 along with three alligators, 50 pheasants, an Asiatic black bear, a goral, a serow, a blue sheep and a vulture. But although given a bed of ice and shaved of much of her hair to protect her from the heat, Jennie lay dead before the ship reached Saigon. Tangier Smith attributed her death to the lack of roughage in her diet of bread, rice and fruit, and with current knowledge of the susceptibility of giant pandas to intestinal problems in captivity, he may well have been right. At the time, however, the notion met with scepticism, most reports preferring to believe that she succumbed to the mountainous seas and the unbearable heat of the tropics (Anon., 1937b).

Tangier Smith was now ill with tuberculosis, but in spite of his own failing health he refused to be beaten. Back in England he horrified family and friends by his determination to return to China and try again. He made his intentions clear in his interview for BBC radio in October 1937:

> I have not yet finished with the business of capturing pandas. I expect to return to China in the very near future, and when I do it will be to go all out for bigger and better pandas.

After resting briefly, Tangier Smith began what was to be his last attempt to bring a panda back to England. After the frustration and disappointment of his previous trip, his luck began to change. By early April 1938 he had captured four animals, three of them males (*New York Times*, 4 Apr. 1938), and according to one Shanghai newspaper was already *en route* from Chengdu to Hong Kong with the animals by 11 April. But something must have happened to change his plans, for three months later he was in Chongqing trying to charter a Douglas airliner to carry a cargo of animals and birds, among them five giant pandas, to Hong Kong (*North China Herald*, 6 July

1938). Finally, on 5 October he was once again in Chongqing, this time with six pandas and an assortment of other game which included the first golden monkey ever to leave the country. Again, no air transport was available, and instead of trying to fly them out he arranged for a convoy of lorries to take the menagerie overland to Hong Kong in the charge of his wife Elizabeth. Arduous at the best of times, the journey was made almost impossible by the Sino-Japanese war. Guangzhou had fallen to the Japanese on 12 October and the convoy was forced to make a long detour.

Tangier Smith himself was now seriously ill and by his own admission would have been unable to survive the overland journey. Instead, he flew ahead to make arrangements for the panda's shipment on to England. In all he had secured nine live animals during 1937, three of which had died. A fourth perished only two days out of Chongqing when one of the trucks rolled down an embankment (*Evening Standard*, 23 Dec. 1938), so that when the battered and exhausted convoy arrived in Kowloon after a three-week journey overland and two days in an overloaded tramp in heavy seas, only five remained (Laseby, 1938).

After a short stay in the Kowloon Dogs' Home to recuperate, the pandas were loaded onto the SS *Antennor* on 16 November and arrived in London on Christmas Eve 1938 to become the first of their kind ever to set foot on British soil. Their subsequent history has already been reliably documented.[5] Of the five, two were thought to be male and three female. The animal that appeared to be the oldest, a female named Grandma, contracted double pneumonia and died soon after her arrival. A male named Happy was sold to a German animal dealer and spent six months on a tour of European zoos before being shipped to the United States and sold for $5,000 to the St Louis Zoo shortly before the outbreak of World War II. This left three animals, two subadults named Dopey and Grumpy, and a cub named Baby. These were bought by London Zoo and their names changed to better suit their Chinese origins. Dopey became Sung and Grumpy was renamed Tang. Baby was to be known as Ming, and almost instantly began working the same panda magic on English crowds as Su Lin had done in America. Ideally suited to her role, she was playful and mischievous. Introduced to royalty, she showed all the respect that could be expected of her by attempting to take a bite out of Queen Mary's umbrella.

In England as in America, the panda magic also began to work its spell on the public conscience. The early panda hunters had been considered heroes, the daring and courage of their exploits widely reported. Now, people began to question the morality of killing and kidnapping rare animals for human pleasure. Several letters to *The Times* expressed concern at the techniques being used to trap pandas. No less a zoologist than Julian Huxley came to Tangier Smith's defence, declaring himself satisfied that pandas were being treated humanely and were not sufficiently rare to cause concern. But doubts remained. In a letter to *The Times* for 17 June 1939, H. Courtney Brocklehurst, the ex-game warden of the Sudan and to this day one of only three Westerners to shoot a wild panda, quoted at length from an article by Arthur Sowerby, editor of the *China Journal* and a naturalist with considerable experience of Chinese wildlife.

We would like to suggest that this business of capturing live pandas for export is already seriously threatening the species with extermination. Reports have reached us that throughout the whole area inhabited by giant pandas the native hunters are scouring the country in search of these animals as well as setting traps for them. Already, according to Mrs. Harkness, who was in that area last spring, two big valleys in the Wassu country, which formerly contained many pandas, have been completely denuded of these animals. Other reports indicate that many pandas, old and young, brought alive to Cheng-tu by native hunters have died there before they could be shipped out of the country, while many more skins of dead ones have been offered for sale in this city, showing that an intensive hunting of giant pandas is going on. A rare and not too plentiful animal at best, the giant panda cannot long survive such persecution, and we strongly urge the Chinese authorities to take measures to protect this and other species of rare animals and birds in China against what can only be described as wholesale commercial exploitation.

By the time this letter was published in England, action had already been taken in China. On 24 April 1939 the Provincial Government of Sichuan issued an order prohibiting the capture of giant pandas. For Western adventurers, the age of panda-hunting was over, but American zoos were not about to give up their quest for a breeding pair.

With Su Lin dead and both Mei Mei and Pandora presumed to be female, the Bronx and Chicago Zoos were still desperate to find mates for their charges. At first it seemed as though they might be lucky, for the ban was flexibly interpreted in respect of animals destined for 'reputable scientific institutions'. In May, through their contacts in Chengdu, the Bronx Zoo secured a young male and was allowed to export him to America. However, unlike the previous animals, Pandora's prospective mate, named Pan, had been captured not as a cub but as a subadult and weighed 32 kg on his arrival at the zoo. Perhaps partly for this reason he was less friendly than the previous pandas, but whether this would have affected his behaviour as a mate to Pandora the zoo never had a chance to discover for both animals died before reaching maturity.

In the autumn of 1939 a third panda arrived at Brookfield Zoo, this time secured by A. T. Steele, a journalist for the *Chicago Daily News*, through his contacts with the staff at the West China Union University. But yet again, there was to be no successful mating, because although Mei Lan lived to the ripe old age of 15, Mei Mei died in 1942 before reaching maturity. Even had they both survived, they would have been incompatible partners since although they were both thought to be females on arrival in Chicago, both eventually turned out to be males.

The ban on export of pandas from China was relaxed once more, in November 1939, allowing the young female Pao Pei to be sent to America. This animal had been bought in Chengdu as an investment by a worker with the Lockheed Aircraft Corporation, Bill Schultz, and sold to St Louis Zoo. By this time the Japanese controlled the whole of eastern China, and Pao Pei spent some time in Chongqing—now the capital of 'Free China'. She was besieged alternately by Nationalist bureaucrats and the Japanese air force—before permission for her export to Hong Kong could be arranged. During several of the air raids the panda was taken into a dugout, where according to *The Times* 'its playful embraces in the darkness increased the thrills but not the pleasures of some of the other inmates' (*The Times*, 9 Aug. 1939). In St Louis she joined one of Tangier Smith's five pandas, the male named Happy.

Pao Pei was the last panda to be captured and exported from China at the behest of Westerners. World War II forced European zoos to abandon their attempts, and the situation in China itself made travel to and from panda country more difficult than ever. None the less, Dr David Graham of the West China Union University was persuaded by Mme Chiang Kai-shek to try to obtain a panda for presentation to the American people in appreciation for their donations to China through the United China Relief fund. An ex-preacher, Den Wei-han, was employed for the task. He had previously been largely responsible for the trapping of both Pan and Pandora, and after some difficulty not one but two pandas were captured. The animals spent some time in Chengdu before being flown across war-torn China to Chongqing and on to the Bronx Zoo via Hong Kong, the Phillipines, Hawaii and San Francisco. In New York they were christened Pan Dee and Pan Dah, and since they were thought to be male and female there were hopes that the pair would mate. Yet again it was not until the animals died—Pan Dee in October 1945 and Pan Dah in October 1951—that their true sex was known for certain. This time, both turned out to be females.

By the end of World War II only five pandas remained alive outside China: Happy, Pao Pei, Mei Lan, Pan Dee and Pan Dah. The death of Ming at London Zoo in December 1944 had left Europe without a single live specimen. Chiang Kai-shek still held power in China, and with the surrender of the Japanese to the Americans in August 1945 a semblance of order returned briefly to west China. Nevertheless, the chances of London or any other zoo obtaining a panda looked fairly slim, since almost all the Europeans that had instigated previous expeditions had left the country. Professor Edward Hindle, director of the London Zoo, pointed out this unfortunate state of affairs to George Yeh of the Chinese embassy one night over dinner, and he promised to see what could be done. A few months later, on 11 May 1946, a male panda arrived at Poole Airport in southern England, presented by General Chang Chun the governor of Sichuan province. Given the Chinese name of Lien Ho, which translates into English as Unity, the animal had been captured by a young Chinese zoologist named Ma Teh, who received a year's fellowship to study in England in return for this gesture of goodwill by the Chinese. But like Pan before him, Lien Ho had been captured as a subadult, and proved to be a surly and unappealing exhibit.

General Chang attempted to repeat the gesture and supply a second panda to the Bronx Zoo in New York as a replacement for Pan Dee, who died in October 1945. An animal was captured in October 1946, but died of acute dysentery in Shanghai before reaching its destination (Anon., 1946). For a while there was hope that attempts would be made to secure another specimen, but China was already entering a new period of civil war which ended in 1949 with the formation of the People's Republic of China by

1. Fir forest at 3000 metres in the Wolong reserve. Although many trees along this ridge were felled before the reserve was established in 1975, giant and red pandas still forage in the bamboo understory. *(Bruce Coleman/WWF/Timm Rautert)*

2. Giant panda habitat in the Qionglai mountains, with rhododendron growing beneath a canopy of fir and birch. The ground is covered by a dense stand of arrow bamboo. In the foreground, the bamboo has flowered and died. Behind it is a small patch of the same species that has yet to flower and still provides food for pandas. *(WWF/D. Reid)*

4. Bamboo flowers. The anthers hanging from the spikelets are typical of grasses. *(Chris Catton)*

Mao Zedong. It was to be ten years before another panda left China bound for a Western zoo.

When Mei Lan died in Brookfield Zoo in 1953, not a single giant panda remained alive in captivity anywhere in the world, including China. Its status in the wild was completely unknown, and the trickle of information that had previously flowed from China dried up completely.

From the moment it first became known to the West, the giant panda has been the subject of controversy. The publicity which followed Su Lin's arrival in the USA and the subsequent debate on the ethics of capturing rare animals for captivity served to sharpen a public debate which is still continuing. It is impossible to untangle the web of cause and effect and decide how much the change in our attitudes towards other animals has been influenced by this endearing creature. The progression from scientific collecting through game hunting to the 'bring 'em back alive' philosophy of collectors like Ruth Harkness may simply reflect a shift in attitudes towards the treatment of wild animals generally. Whatever part the giant panda played in bringing about that shift, by the time Chi Chi arrived in London Zoo in 1957, another change was already well under way. Zoos were still almost universally regarded as respectable scientific institutions, but the growing awareness of the scale of environmental degradation was already fuelling increasingly vociferous calls for the conservation of the animal in its natural habitat.

Notes

1. Beijing was until recently transliterated as Peking, but for consistency I have used the modern pinyin spellings for Chinese place names throughout this book.
2. Twenty-five francs is what he later told Milne-Edwards.
3. Several authors have cast doubt on the association between Smith and Harkness, but their departure and return were both recorded in the contemporary press. See, for example, 'The Harkness Expedition', *China Journal 23* (1935):19, and 'Harkness and Smith Return', *China Journal 23* (1935):221.
4. The village which Ruth Harkness calls Tsaopo.
5. For a more detailed account see Morris and Morris (1966).

2. Panda Country

The mountains around the Tibetan plateau are among the most awesome on earth. In the Himalayas to the south and west rise many of the world's highest peaks, including several that reach over 8,000 m. To the east the earth's crust is less dramatically distorted, although there are still peaks like Minya Konka which at 7,590 m dwarfs all mountains beyond the Asian continent. These mountains have been created by events that rate as recent on the geological time-scale. Somewhere between about 40 and 50 million years ago the Indian landmass collided with the Asian continent, buckling and contorting itself to form the Himalayas and raising what had once been the floor of the Tethys sea to create the Tibetan plateau. With the coming of the ice-age, animals unable to cope with the climatic changes elsewhere in the continent found refuge on the slopes of this vast plateau. As great glaciers pushed down the mountains from the north and west, they moved to lower altitudes, returning to the mountains as the earth warmed again.

In these unique conditions, trapped between the ice and the subtropical forests of the lowland plains, many Pleistocene species survived to flourish as the ice retreated. To the east of the Tibetan plateau the forces of this great collision raised sedimentary rocks laid down in ancient seas to create many of the mountains that now encircle the Sichuan plain. In a landscape of towering peaks and plunging valleys shrouded for much of the year in mist and cloud, porcupines, takin, yellow-throated marten, hog badger, wild pig and sambar deer, have adapted to life in the rugged mountain strongholds where they now cling to a precarious existence on the forested cliffs and the high alpine meadows. Here they have been joined by other creatures that have successfully invaded the area since the ice-sheets retreated—among them the golden pheasant, serow, and clouded leopard—to create an ecosystem found nowhere else in the world. In one single reserve there are over 4,000 species of native plants, more than in the whole of Europe. No less than nine different species of pheasant inhabit the mountains of western Sichuan: Temminck's tragopan with its fiery orange breast and crown and bright blue face; the Chinese monal, with its glittering plumage, the head shining iridescent blue-green while the back and sides glint coppery purple; the white-eared and blue-eared pheasants, the golden pheasant, Lady Amherst's pheasant, the koklass pheasant and the blood pheasant are all native to the same mountains.

In the mixed broad-leaved and conifer forests high in the mountains, rare golden monkeys feed on lichens, tree bark, buds and fruit. One afternoon in the Wolong Reserve I sat and watched as a troop of about 200 golden monkeys swung through the tall fir and hemlock trees to cross a deep ravine. They had been disturbed by another of our party higher up the mountain, and the large males, each weighing about 14 kg, sent branches crashing to the forest floor below in a noisy and impressive anti-predator display. Their long golden fur provides essential insulation against the cold, and with their blue faces and distinctive snub-noses they are among the most attractive of all primates. After crossing the ravine the troop reached the safety of a ridge, where the females began to settle down, huddling together for warmth and grooming the young. The males continued with their crashing-display, sometimes leaping from the top of a 30 m fir and breaking several branches as they fell to the ground. None the worse for their ordeal, they immediately began climbing the trees again to repeat the performance.

The same ice-age refugia that protected this remarkable collection of plants and animals also ensured the survival of the giant and red pandas. Of these, the red panda now has much the larger range. With the bamboos and oaks, the species expanded from its ice-age refuge in Sichuan and Yunnan, spreading westwards as the departing glaciers opened new migration routes for both flora and fauna. Moving into the Himalayas it joined other ice-age survivals like the tahr, a primitive goat-antelope, and the Impeyan monal, now the national bird of Nepal. Until recently the red panda could be found wherever there was suitable habitat in an arc spreading from northern India, through Nepal, Sikkim, Bhutan, northern Burma and into the Chinese provinces of Yunnan and Sichuan, and the south-eastern corner of Tibet itself (Feng *et al.*, 1981).

The giant panda has never, as far as is known, succeeded in colonising the western area of the red panda's range, and is now restricted to the mountains along the eastern edge of the Tibetan plateau. Although centred on western Sichuan, the giant panda's range spreads across three provinces. In Shaanxi province a population estimated in 1974 to be around 200 animals survives on the southern slopes of the Qinling mountains, homeland of the Qin Emperor, the tyrannical despot who first united China into a single country. To the north of the Qinling mountains, the emperor lies buried beneath the old Qin capital of Xianyang, along with his escort of thousands of terracotta soldiers.

Evidence of giant pandas in the Qinling mountains was first obtained in the mid-1880s by the Russian explorers Berezovski and Potanin (Büchner, 1892), who brought back several skins purchased from native hunters, one of which found its way to the British Museum of Natural History in London. This area is isolated from the rest of the panda's range, and it was not until 1964 that the existence of this population was confirmed with a specimen obtained by Chinese researchers.

Several hundred kilometres to the west lie the Min mountains, where along the border between Gansu and Sichuan lives a second, larger population of animals. South of this, the Qionglai mountains tower above the western bank of the Min river. These contain the third patch of panda country, where Père David collected his specimens, and where Su Lin and most of the pandas that followed her were captured. South again lie three small panda ranges, centred on the Daxiang, Xiaoxiang, and Liang mountains.

The range of the giant panda was once much larger. Biochemical studies (discussed in detail in Chapter 4) show that the giant panda split from the bear lineage between 20 million and 25 million years ago. Fossils from this period suggest that the most likely candidate as a panda ancestor is a small, dog-sized bear, *Ursavus*, from which all bears appear to be derived. From *Ursavus*, the fossil bear *Agriarctos* evolved in the mid-Miocene, already with specialised, flattened cheek teeth, but truly panda-like animals do not

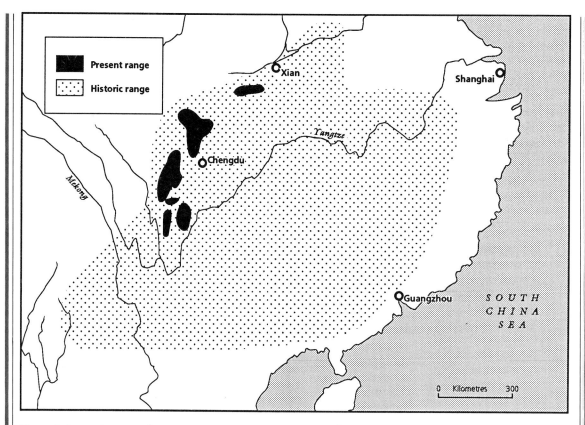

Figure 2. Past and present range of the giant panda.

appear in the fossil record until the early Pleistocene, the most recent of the geological epochs which began some 1.8 million years ago (Thenius, 1979). These were about half the size of present day pandas, and have been classified as a separate and now extinct species, *Ailuropoda microta*. We know little about this animal's range or habits, for the species is known only from a single cave in Guangxi province (Wang, 1974), but judging by the structure of its skull and teeth, this animal was already adapted to a bamboo diet. By the mid-Pleistocene, roughly one million years ago, animals indistinguishable from modern giant pandas were widespread (Zhu and Long, 1983). Fossils have been collected throughout China, from Beijing south across the eastern plains, and west to Kunming. Most of these fossils have been found on hilly ground, although it is unclear whether this reflects a preference for a particular type of habitat or simply poor preservation of the remains in the alluvial plains. In the mid-Pleistocene, the panda's range even extended into northern Burma, northern Vietnam and Thailand (Woodward, 1915; Ciochon, 1988; and Ginsburg *et al.*, 1982). During the Pleistocene, the climate throughout the northern hemisphere changed several times, with cold ice-ages separated by spells of comparatively warm weather. Probably the panda's range expanded and contracted several times during this period, but the fossil record suggests that the last decline began perhaps 10,000–20,000 years ago. This coincides roughly with the end of the last ice-age, and no doubt as the earth warmed pandas were forced to higher altitudes as the plains were covered by a dense forest ill suited to the growth of bamboo. Bamboo is relatively scarce in the subtropical forest that now grows to the south of the giant panda's present range, and the *Chimnocalamus* species that do manage to grow in these forests are probably unpalatable to pandas (Campbell and Qin, 1983). They are thorny and have a yellow, aromatic and insect-repellent sap, defences that plants typically employ to discourage grazing animals. Early this century, remnants of this lowland forest around Shanghai still contained tigers, but the elephant and tapir probably disappeared from central China about 2,000 years ago, at about the same time that the rhinoceros (*Rhinoceros sondaicus*) became extinct in China.

It is likely that the lowland subtropical forest was never suitable panda habitat, and the only recent records of pandas from subtropical forest south of the present known range are extremely doubtful. For example, photographs taken of a 'panda' shot in the Salween district of Burma on the border with Siam and sent to the English newspaper the *Morning Post* in 1936 by one Major Phipps, clearly show the animal in question to be an Asiatic black bear.

The mountains that ring the Sichuan plain still provide a huge area of potential habitat for these animals, but there are more than enough scattered historical records to be certain that the panda's range has shrunk dramatically in the last 2,000 years, due entirely to the effect of human disturbance as agriculture began to dominate Sichuan and the surrounding provinces. In 1866 pandas still inhabited the Wu Shan region of western Hubei (Zhu and Long, 1983), well to the east of the current range. In 1930 pandas were reported to be pests in the southern Qionglai mountains, and along with brown and Asiatic black bears were blamed for raiding crops (Kilborn, 1965). As recently as 1948 there were still pandas on Mount Emei near Leshan, but in recent years sightings from this area have all been doubtful. Pandas have now disappeared even from the old 'Kingdom of Wassu' where many of the pandas that found their way to Western zoos were collected in the 1930s and 40s.

To the west of the present range lies the Tibetan plateau, and despite reports to the contrary it is unlikely that pandas have lived here in recent times. In 1940 members of the Natural Resources Exploration Expedition reported seeing a mother and her two cubs near Tsaring-Nor in Qinghai province, at least 282 km west of the nearest-known panda country. Although the party had a good view of the animals, there are many reasons to doubt that these were pandas. According to Hung Shou Pen, who later reported the sighting (Pen, 1943), the two cubs followed the mother and suckled her 'as does a little pig or calf'. It is extremely rare, although not unknown, for a panda to raise two cubs in a single year, and pandas in captivity do not suckle in this way. The mother was also feeding on gentians, irises, crocuses, Chinese vines and tufted grasses, and although it is known that pandas do occasionally eat plants other than bamboo, such catholic tastes certainly suggest another case of mistaken identity. Hung Shou Pen was a competent zoologist, but his report notes that the female's fur was 'sparklingly bright as the sun shone upon it'. Even the best field observers can be fooled by a trick of the light, and it is more than likely that the animals in question were actually brown bears.

In 1966 it was reported in Beijing that pandas had been captured in the 'Tibetan Himalayas', and that they were 'similar to those found in the bamboo groves of Szechwan Province, once thought to be the only place they existed' (Anon., 1966). This would have extended the known range considerably, and would also have given some credibility to earlier suggestions that the giant panda and the abominable snowman might be one and the same. In fact, when the animals arrived at Beijing Zoo they turned out to be red pandas (Heuvelmans, 1966). It seems most likely that the confusion was the result of an error in translation.

With the desolate Tibetan plateau to the west, the intensively farmed Sichuan plain to the east, the subtropical forests of Yunnan and Burma to the south, and the deserts of Gansu to the north, the giant panda is now surrounded. John Mackinnon, a zoologist working on the panda project, eloquently stated the panda's present situation in the conclusion of his report to the World Wildlife Fund.

> Today the panda is in its last stronghold. It has nowhere else to go. Westward lies only the rock and ice of the Tibetan plateau, where pandas have never lived. The panda literally has its back against the wall. (Mackinnon and Qiu, 1986)

Although like the giant panda confined to temperate forests with a

Figure 3. Approximate historic range of the red panda.

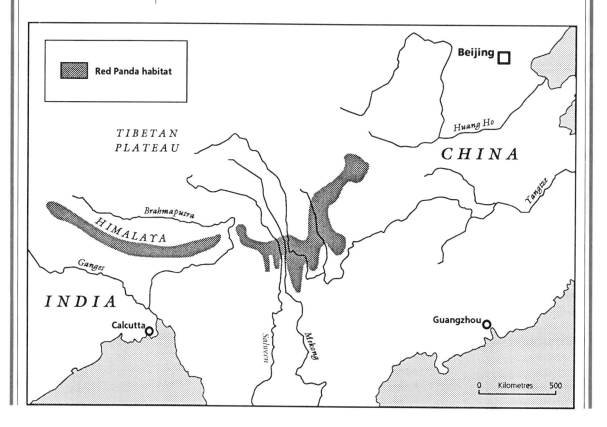

bamboo under-storey, the red panda is much more widely distributed. Its northern and eastern limits are roughly coincident with the range of the giant panda, but the red panda can be found as far west as the Namlung valley in western Nepal, and as far south as the Liakiang range of western Yunnan (Roberts and Gittleman, 1984).

During the Pleistocene the red panda was confined to a small refugium in western Sichuan and Yunnan, and even during the ice-ages it appears that the lowland plains were never suitable habitat.[1] But the fossil history of the red panda can be traced back to the Oligocene and early Miocene epochs, more than 25 million years ago, when the racoon-like ancestors of the red panda were distributed throughout the northern temperate zone. Among these various animals, the earliest indisputably panda-like fossils are those of the several *Sivanasua* species, known only from a few teeth and broken jawbones. Fossils of the extinct red panda *Parailurus*, which was larger than the modern red panda, have been found in England, Europe and even North America, and there may have been at least three different species living in the northern hemisphere between 3 and 4 million years ago. Of these fossil forms, only the specialised red panda survived the Pleistocene glaciations, probably in the same mountain ranges in which the giant panda found refuge as the climate changed and changed again.

At the end of the last ice-age, the red panda moved west, expanding into its present range. But as the ice retreated and the red pandas were forced higher into the mountains, the populations in Sichuan, Yunnan and Burma became isolated from the Himalayan population, in part by the torrential rivers that cut increasingly deep gorges through the mountains as they carried the melting snows from the Tibetan plateau to the Indian Ocean. Now these two separate populations are recognised as distinct subspecies, the dividing line being the particularly wide and deep valley cut through the mountains by the Brahmaputra river. Animals from the eastern end of the range tend to be slightly heavier, with more robust dentition, thicker, rather darker fur, and bolder markings. First made known to the West in 1897 by F. W. Styan, this subspecies has been given the scientific name *Ailurus fulgens styani*, and is commonly known as Styan's panda. With the exception of the Qinling mountains, Styan's panda is found wherever there are giant pandas, although differences in the feeding behaviour of the two species dictate that Styan's panda rarely descends to the valley bottoms, and can live at slightly higher altitudes than the giant panda.

Anyone reading the reports of the first Western game-hunters and trappers is left in no doubt that the giant panda lives in some of the darkest, densest, and most forbidding jungle to be found anywhere in the world. The vivid description by Theodore and Kermit Roosevelt (1929) is typical:

> After walking a couple of miles down the valley, we turned into the mountains. At once we found ourselves in the densest jungle I have ever known. It was of bamboo six to eight feet tall, interspersed with hemlock and beech. The slope was forty-five degrees. We had to climb on hands and knees. Deadfall blocked us every few feet. The dust from the dead bamboo leaves got into our lungs and eyes. The stems and matted vines through which we have to force our way tripped and

clung to us like the tentacles of an octopus. The sweat ran in streams and caked the dust. It was impossible to see twenty feet.

These stories are exaggerated, as befits an age when hunters were expected to be good tellers of tales and not to spoil the flow of their prose style with too close an attention to detail. Although the terrain is difficult, with many mountains over 4,500 m, steep slopes, and deep valleys, the vegetation is not as unremittingly impenetrable as those early accounts suggest. At the upper limits of the giant panda's altitudinal range, around 3,400 m, the forest is actually quite open, with only a relatively sparse covering of bamboo beneath the dense canopy of firs. The bamboos that grow at these altitudes are generally slender plants, with stems rarely more than a metre tall and no thicker than a pencil. A few rhododendrons grow scattered throughout the forest, adding bright splashes of colour in spring, but these rarely form the impossible tangles of the rhododendron thickets at higher altitude. Fallen trees, a thick carpet of moss, and centuries of forest debris all combine to slow progress, but in open areas with no bamboo, and along deer trails, walking would be easy if the hills were not so steep.

Lower down, the conifers are mixed with deciduous trees—maple, basswood, paper birch and cherry, and the firs are replaced by hemlocks and spruces. Here the forest is denser. Taller bamboo species, like the umbrella bamboo (*Fargesia robusta*) which grows to a height of 2.5–3 m, replace the shorter-growing species that dominate at higher altitude. This bamboo really is unpleasant to move through, since the tangled live stems must constantly be pushed aside, while dead stems on the ground are treacherously slippery, but rarely does the bamboo cover an area so large that there is no way around it. Outside the stands of bamboo, thick layers of leaves carpet the ground. With wood sorrel, ferns and delicate purple-flowered primulas growing beneath hazel and rhododendron, parts of this forest have the look of an English woodland—albeit tilted at an outrageous angle.

Below about 2,000 m the character of the forest changes again, with evergreen oak, birch, maple, dogwood and Chinese walnut being the dominant trees. A wider variety of bamboos grow in this forest, and bamboo thickets are difficult to move through, but once again, large tracts of forest have only a sparse under-storey.

In China the giant panda shares much of its habitat with the red panda, but the red panda's wider geographic range encompasses a wider range of forest types. In Bhutan and Nepal differences in rainfall and temperature across the Himalayas create a patchwork of different forest habitats that meet the animal's basic needs. In the north-west of Nepal between 3,000 and 3,500 m, the dominant species in red panda habitat are firs, oaks and birches, beneath which grows a dense under-storey of rhododendron and ringal bamboo (*Arundinaria spp.*), while at lower altitudes hemlocks replace the first and the rhododendron becomes patchier. To the south, where rainfall is higher, a more complex forest of oaks, firs, hemlocks and birches is mixed with maple, alder and holly, again with ringal bamboo as the red panda's main food source. In the central Himalayan region, which includes Langtang National Park, red pandas inhabit a forest ecosystem dominated by fir (*Abies spectabilis*) and two species of bamboo known

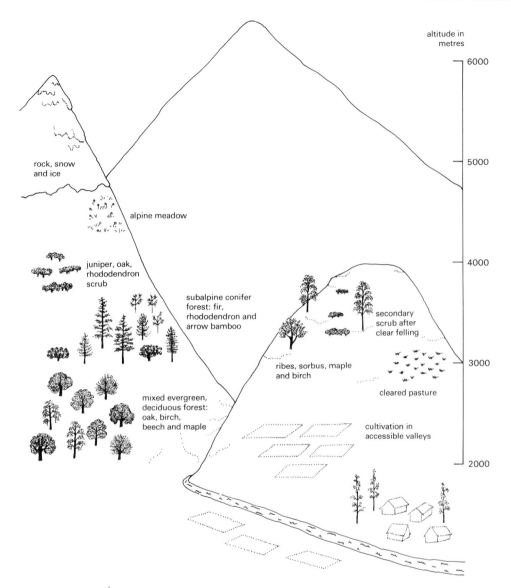

altitude in
metres

6000

rock, snow
and ice

5000

alpine meadow

juniper, oak,
rhododendron
scrub

4000

subalpine conifer
forest: fir,
rhododendron and
arrow bamboo

secondary
scrub after
clear felling

ribes, sorbus, maple
and birch

3000

cleared pasture

mixed evergreen,
deciduous forest:
oak, birch,
beech and maple

cultivation in
accessible valleys

2000

Figure 4. Vegetation types in the Qionglai mountains. Further north in the Min mountains the vegetation is similar, but each zone begins about 300m lower down the mountains.

locally as jhapra and raate (both *Arundinaria* spp.)[2] (Yonzon and Hunter, 1989), Jhapra grows to a height of about 3 m, with stems that average 1 cm in diameter at the base, while raate is rather sturdier, with stem diameters of 1.5 cm and an average height of about 4 m. To the east of Nepal, conifers are scarcer, and the broadleaf forest is dominated by laurels, oaks and castanopsis trees. This broadleaf forest extends eastward into Bhutan, and here there is a high enough rainfall to support the growth of a mixed fir, hemlock and birch forest at higher altitude. Beneath this mixed canopy grows malling bamboo, *Arundinaria cf. malling*, which again provides a suitable food source for the red pandas.

Throughout the range of both panda species, the lower limit of their habitat is now usually defined by the encroachment of fields and livestock. The vast patchwork of rice-paddies that feed the bulk of Asia's population, long ago drove most wild creatures from fertile areas like the Sichuan plain and the Kathmandu valley. Higher in the mountains the progress of agricultural expansion has been slower, hampered by the climate, the poor soil and the near impossibility of scratching a living from the often precipitous mountainsides. Throughout the mountains, many of the peoples who now farm these valleys trace their ancestry to Tibet, where farming conditions are if anything even more difficult. Their racial background is evident both in their features and their dress, many still retaining the same elaborate traditional costume they have worn for centuries. As recently as the 1940s many of these farmers were desperately poor. Leslie Kilborn, who travelled through the area during the 1930s, wrote 'it is the only place in China where I have seen Chinese women so poverty-stricken that some of the adult women were completely naked' (Kilborn, 1965). Now, roads have been cut through the mountains, bringing trade, law enforcement, and with it a limited prosperity. Solid stone houses with shingled roofs have replaced the thatched hovels seen by early travellers.

Throughout the mountains the crops are much the same: wheat, buckwheat, potatoes and turnips, with maize and beans grown during the brief warmth of the summer months. Goats, sheep, yak and dzo (a hybrid between yak and cattle) are grazed on the higher pastures, pushing the pandas ever higher up into the mountains. The expansion of agriculture has threatened the survival of both panda species, and the loss of habitat to agriculture has been aggravated by the felling of trees on higher slopes for fuel and timber.

If the lower limit of the giant panda's altitudinal range is now defined by the encroachment of fields and livestock, the upper limit is defined as it always was, by the growth of bamboo. Above the firs, at about 3,400 m, gnarled and eerie tangles of rhododendron and juniper scrub open into meadows that in spring are alive with alpine flowers—Himalayan poppies, primroses, gentians, fritillaries and orchids. In the south of the panda's range bamboo still grows at this altitude, but it is short and stunted, often reaching no higher than 45 cm above the ground. This is useless to giant pandas, and only exceptionally do they move to this altitude to cross a ridge into another area. However, this habitat can still support red pandas, which have been recorded up to 4,800 m in some areas.

To try to stem the tide of destruction, nature reserves have been established to protect the habitat of both the red and giant pandas. In China the first of these reserves to be officially designated were at Baihe in the northern Min mountains, and Labaihe in the south of the Qionglai range, both set up in 1963, followed in 1965 by Wanglang, also in the Min mountains. Wolong, the largest, and thanks to the work of the China/World Wildlife Fund Giant Panda Project, undoubtedly the most famous, is considered to be of such importance that it has been listed as an International Biosphere Reserve. Although it was not declared a reserve until 1973, it also has an unofficial claim to precedence. Long ago, according to local legend, a young and beautiful girl lived in the Wolong valley with her family. She was a shepherdess, loved by all who knew her for her kindness and good nature.

Whenever she took her sheep into the hills a young panda would come to join her flock, perhaps mistaking them for its own kind for in those days pandas were all white.

One day the panda arrived as usual, but it had not been playing with the flock for long when a leopard jumped from a tree and began to savage the helpless cub. Careless of her own life, the girl picked up a stick and began to beat the leopard. The panda ran off, but the leopard turned on its attacker and killed her.

When the other pandas heard this, they were stricken with grief. All came to attend the girl's funeral, and as a mark of their respect they covered their arms with ashes as was the custom. At the funeral, they could not contain themselves. They wiped their eyes to dry their tears, and hugged themselves as they sobbed. The cries became so loud that they covered their ears with their paws to block out the noise. Wherever they touched themselves the ashes stained their fur black and since that day all pandas have carried these marks.

Overcome with sorrow, the girl's three sisters threw themselves into her grave, whereupon the earth shook and in place of the grave a huge mountain appeared. That mountain still stands, and is called Siguniang—the four sisters mountain. Each sister was transformed into one of its four peaks, and between the ridges that spread from it the sisters continue to protect the pandas to this day.

I suspected that this might be a story recently written for visitors to the reserve, but was assured by local people that they had heard it on their mothers' knee as children. In a sense it is true that the mountains once protected the animals, their very presence making the area almost totally inaccessible except to the most determined travellers. Now, roads have been cut deep into the panda's habitat, and its future in the wild is uncertain. Increasingly it is the boundaries of reserves and not the mountains themselves that offer protection to the pandas.

A total of twelve reserves have now been established, together covering an area of over 5,000 km² (see Table 2.1).

The current status of the red panda is poorly known throughout its present range. In Nepal the red panda is probably close to extinction outside the Langtang and Sagarmatha National Parks, and the proposed Annapurna conservation area, although there may also be small populations in the Rara National Park and in the newly formed Shey-phoksumdo National Park (Bhatt, 1977). It is no longer found in eastern Kashmir, Sikkim and Assam (Roberts, 1982b). Dhorpatan contains suitable habitat, as does the Barun valley which is a proposed extension of the Sagarmatha National Park, and these areas have been so little studied that other populations may yet be found here. In northern Burma the red panda is now rare and is not afforded any official protection, although under the Forest Act, no forest product (including wildlife) can legally be taken out of the forest reserves (Glatston, 1980). A park has been proposed in Kachin state in the extreme north of Burma which would conserve an area of suitable habitat in which a few animals probably still survive, but at the time of writing the war of attrition between Burmese government forces and the guerillas camped in these

Table 2.1 Panda reserves in China

Name	District	Province	Year	Area (km²)	No. of pandas	No. of local people in reserve
Baihe	Nanping	Sichuan	1963	200	20	0
Labaihe	Tianquan	Sichuan	1963	120	25	?
Wanglang	Pingwu	Sichuan	1965	277	10–20	0
Fengtongzhai	Baoxing	Sichuan	1975	400	50	2,000
Wolong	Wenchuan	Sichuan	1975	2,000	72	3,000
Dafengding	Mabian	Sichuan	1978	300	30–40	0
Dafengding	Meigu	Sichuan	1978	160	10	2,000
Tangjiahe	Qingchuan	Sichuan	1978	400	100–140	0
Jiuzhaigou	Nanping	Sichuan	1978	600	40	820
Baishuijiang	Wen	Gansu	1978	953	20–25	10,000
Xiaozhaizigou	Beichuan	Sichuan	1979	167	20	0
Foping	Foping	Shaanxi	1980	350	40	200–300

From Schaller (1985), with adjustments where more recent data is available.

same mountains looks likely to forestall any attempt at wildlife conservation in the area (Blower, 1985). In Bhutan the status of the red panda is unknown, but much of the primary forest remains and it is likely that a healthy population still survives.

Early travellers into panda country may have bolstered their egos with their descriptions of the vegetation, but the difficulties they faced in dealing with the climate really were formidable. Totally ill-equipped by modern standards, they spent weeks or months cold and soaking wet. It is not that the rainfall is particularly high—in giant panda habitat the mean annual rainfall is probably no more than a metre a year, although there are no accurate, long-term data. Even in the wet season between March and September as the monsoon lashes south-eastern China and dies over the mountains, rainfall at 2,500 m averages only about 150 cm a month. But the dampness is ever present. Constantly swirling mists and clouds keep the forest dripping wet, and pushing through tall bamboos brings down a shower of water that quickly soaks everything. In winter overnight snow often leaves the air so clear that every detail can be seen on distant mountains that cut like sharp flints into the blue sky. In the open these days are wonderfully dry, and even feel warm in the winter sun, but beneath the forest canopy the sun soon melts the snow on the trees and the endless dripping begins once again.

This constantly wet environment seems to be essential for the growth of bamboo, and without the bamboo there would of course be no pandas. There are over 1,200 species of bamboo in the world, of which perhaps 300 are native to China—the taxonomy of bamboos is in such chaos that no two authorities come close to agreeing on a number. In habit these range from giant woody plants reaching heights of 20 or 30 m through low-growing

Figure 5. China's giant panda reserves.

shrubs to delicate dwarf varieties. A few are even scrambling climbers. Bamboo is central to Chinese culture, used to make baskets, furniture, mats, boxes, tools, musical instruments, paper, rope, ladders, medicines and chopsticks—the list is endless. In high-tech Hong Kong, a scaffold of bamboo stems embraces even the tallest and most futuristic construction projects, not simply because it is cheaper than aluminium scaffolding, but because it will not collapse in a typhoon.

Table 2.2 Red panda reserves

Name	Year	Area (km²)
Langtang	1976	1,710
Lake Rara	1976	106
Sagarmatha	1976	1,148
Shey-phoksumdo	1984	3,555
Dhorpatan	1987	1,325
Annapurna		2,660

Data on Nepalese reserves from: Carol Inskipp
'Nepal's forest birds: Their status and conservation',
International council for bird preservation
monograph no. 4, ICBP, Cambridge, UK, 1989.

Bamboo is a grass, though from an animal's point of view it is an unusually tough one to eat. The stems are woody, and the leaves are unpalatable to many grazing animals. Only the shoots are easily digested. Soft and fleshy, these are the 'bamboo shoots' of Chinese cookery, nutritious and high in fibre. They are harvested both by men and animals as they poke through the soil from the network of rhizomes that grow beneath its surface. The sheaths that surround each shoot are little protection against the squirrels, pikas, takin, deer, insects, people and pandas that feed on them. Yet the harvest is short. In the mountains of Sichuan most shoots emerge during the first days of spring and then develop at an incredible pace. Shoots of some of the larger species can grow well over a metre in 24 hours. Shoots of the umbrella bamboo (*Fargesia robusta*), important as food for pandas, can grow 18 cm in a single day, spearing dead leaves as they force their way out of the soil and lifting them high into the air. Within six weeks the shoots are tall and becoming woody, and most animals switch back to other, easier fodder.

For many animals the bamboo shoots provide a short seasonal supplement to their diet. The few animals that specialise in feeding on bamboo must also be able to digest the tough leaves or stems, but it is another of the plants' defences that causes most problems to these creatures. Some bamboo species grow to maturity and then flower and seed every year, just like any other grass. A few short-growing Himalayan types do this, and so do some tropical species. Most, however, including the species on which the pandas depend for their food, give no indication of flowering for many years. Then in one spectacular burst of reproductive energy all the plants over a vast area begin to sprout the delicate panicles typical of grasses. For a short while the air is loaded with pollen, and with the last of their energy the plants set seed, usually producing a heavy crop. Within a few months the forest is transformed. In place of the dense cover of the bamboo understorey only the dry, sharp stems remain standing, for once these strange plants have flowered, they die.

Reports of mass flowerings in China go back more than 2,000 years. In the *Shau Hai Jing*—the 'Record of the Natural World'—it was noted that 'if

5. a. and b. *Above and right* Young pandas climb trees to escape from predators and to avoid others of their own kind. *(WWF/Dr K. Mackinnon; China Tourist Service Co.)*

6. A giant panda moving through bamboo in the Wolong reserve. Pandas typically save their energy by keeping to level ground where possible and avoiding the steeper slopes (WWF/Timm Rautert)

7. Zhen Zhen feeding on arrow bamboo leaves. This old female was the first to be trapped and fitted with a radio collar, and eventually became fairly tolerant of humans. *(Ken Johnson)*

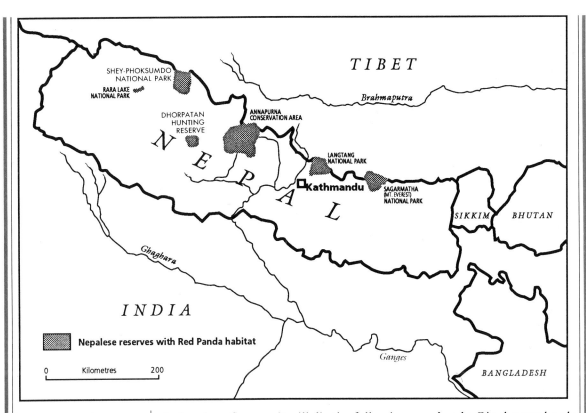

TIBET

Brahmaputra

SHEY-PHOKSUMDO NATIONAL PARK

RARA LAKE NATIONAL PARK

DHORPATAN HUNTING RESERVE

ANNAPURNA CONSERVATION AREA

N E P A L

LANGTANG NATIONAL PARK

Kathmandu

SAGARMATHA (MT. EVEREST) NATIONAL PARK

SIKKIM   BHUTAN

Ghaghara

I N D I A

Nepalese reserves with Red Panda habitat

0   Kilometres   200

Ganges

BANGLADESH

Figure 6. Nepalese reserves with suitable habitat for red pandas.

the bamboo flowers, it will die the following year,' and a Qin dynasty book on bamboo by Dai Kai recorded flowering on a 60-year cycle (Wen and Wang, 1980). Detailed records of the flowering of economically important species like the giant timber bamboo (*Phyllostachys bambusoides*) go back many centuries. According to documents in Chinese temples, the giant timber bamboo flowered in AD 999 (Kawamura, 1927) and again in AD 1114. Other records for this species indicate that it flowers regularly every 120 years. This is an unusually long flowering cycle, even for bamboo, though many other species wait for 40 to 50 years before their one frantic burst of sexual reproduction. Of the species that are important to pandas as food, the arrow bamboo, *Gelidocalamus fangianus* has a flowering period of between 42 and 48 years, and *Fargesia nitida*, the sword bamboo, a flowering period of around 70 to 80 years.

The flowering period of each bamboo species appears to be genetically determined, since cuttings transplanted to very different environments thousands of kilometres apart usually come into flower at the same time as their parents. When *Arundinaria japonica* flowered in Japan in 1867 and 1868, so did cuttings transplanted to the Bois de Boulogne, Sceaux, Marseilles and Algiers. There are many similar records for other species although the story is not always the same. Some species may fail to flower in synchrony when transplanted to different climates, suggesting that the underlying genetic clock interacts somehow with environmental conditions, and there is some evidence that drought may help to trigger flowering. The flowering of *Fargesia denudata* and *F. scabrida* in the Min mountains in 1975 and 1976 marked the beginning of a period of drought which may also have triggered the flowering of *Qiongzhuea rigidula* in southern Sichuan between 1980 and 1981, and the later flowering of arrow bamboo *Gelidocalamus fangianus* and stone bamboo *Yushania chungii* in Wolong. Thanks to the China/World Wildlife Fund Panda Research Project, the flowering in Wolong in 1983 was well documented, and data collected as part of this project show that it was preceded by several years in which rainfall averaged some 20–50 per cent below normal. The rainfall figures are much less reliable for previous flowering events, but there is a marked coincidence between periods of bamboo flowering and periods of relatively low rainfall throughout Sichuan. In the western Himalayas too, there is evidence that droughts tend to occur in regular 33-year cycles, and flowering events tend to follow between one and five years later (Campbell, 1987). Some scientists have suggested that these periods of drought are part of a regular 11-year cycle related to sunspot activity, based on a study of variations in the annual growth rates of trees and the deposition of sedimentary rocks (Campbell and Qin, 1983). Some Chinese workers also suggest that flowering may be triggered by earthquakes. While this seems far-fetched at first sight, earthquakes are often followed by a drop in the water table, and if flowering is triggered in part by drought, then a connection is certainly a possibility. The published evidence for a link between earthquakes, drought and flowering events is weak, but the Chinese have shown recently that their understanding of earthquakes and their ability to predict them is very sophisticated.

Even plants in the same area often fail to come into flower at exactly the same time. It may be that once one plant has flowered, others in the same area are somehow triggered by it, but the tendency for plants to come into flower together is so marked that it is unlikely that communication between plants is a major factor. Because there is some variation between the flowering times of plants of the same species, many botanists quibble with the use of the word 'synchrony', and prefer 'gregarious', a choice which many zoologists who use the word in its more familiar context find uncomfortable. Perhaps 'isochronous', meaning 'equal in intervals of occurrence', would be a better description, but as far as I know, no-one has yet taken up the term. Daniel Janzen, equally discomfited by the not-quite-accurate use of English, has suggested 'mast seeding' (Janzen, 1976) as a suitable alternative, but to avoid proliferating jargon I shall continue to refer to synchronous flowering, with apologies to all botanists whose sensibilities are offended.

Synchronous flowering is obviously important for wind-pollinated plants like bamboo, at least some of which need to be cross pollinated if the seeds are to be fertile. By dying back after flowering, the parent plants allow light to penetrate to the forest floor and release valuable nutrients back into the soil, so giving their seedlings a chance to thrive. But why do most bamboos flower so rarely? It has been suggested that the die-off following flowering provides tinder for forest fires, which open up the canopy above and so let still more light through to the forest floor. This seems an unlikely explanation, at least for the species important to pandas as food. The seedlings of several species require shade in order to develop successfully, and the mountain vegetation is constantly dripping with water throughout the year making fires extremely rare. Another possible explanation is that by dropping a mass of seeds all at once, and then not flowering again for half a century or so, the bamboo successfully avoids losing its seeds to predators (Janzen, 1976). The seeds are very nutritious, containing as much protein as wheat and lacking protective toxins. Some of the tall bamboos can produce an enormous quantity of seed, *Dendrocalamus strictus* yielding an incredible 4 kilos to the square metre. Others are quite unlike typical grasses, but bear fleshy fruits the size of a largish pear. These fall from the tall bamboo poles with such force that at the turn of the century a young British army officer was forced to abandon his survey work in India by the flowering of the giant bamboo *Melocanna bambusoides*. Dropping from over 10 m in the air, the falling fruits kept smashing his instruments (Stapf, 1904).

Such a massive supply of nutritious food attracts a variety of seed-eating animals, and many mass flowerings have been accompanied by an explosion in the population of rats and mice. Birds and squirrels also eat large amounts of seed. Wild pigs gorge themselves, porcupines, elephants, even rhinoceros have all been seen eating the seeds of bamboo, but so overwhelming is the supply of grain that some seeds inevitably survive to germinate. The bloated rodent population returns quickly to its equilibrium level, and the tiny bamboo seedlings slowly begin to set the cycle in motion once again.

Synchronised flowering and seeding of the tall, dense, semi-tropical and tropical species effectively swamps the seed eaters with more food than they can possibly handle, so that some at least is overlooked and survives to germinate and grow. Among the short-growing bamboos typical of the forest under-storey in more temperate climes, seeding is not so overwhelmingly profuse. Large flocks of birds were seen feeding on seed following the flowering of *Fargesia nitida* in 1896 (Bretschneider, 1898), and it may be that the unusually high proportion of umbrella bamboo shoots killed by rodents in Wolong Reserve in 1984 was the result of a minor explosion in the rodent population following the flowering of arrow bamboo higher up the mountain in the previous year (Taylor and Qin, 1987). Reserve workers have also reported an apparent increase in owls and hawks following flowering, presumably preying on an increased but less obvious population of rodents.

Birds and rodents are the most obvious predators on bamboo seed, but they are probably not the most important. During the mass flowering of arrow bamboo in Wolong during 1983, at least 34 per cent of the flowers produced seed. In the few patches that flowered out of synchrony a year later, only 0.6 per cent of the flowers produced seed. The very poor crop of seed in 1984 was almost entirely due to the activity of insects, flies whose larvae had tunnelled into and destroyed the developing ovaries within the flowers (Taylor and Qin, 1988b).

While saturation of seed predators is an important evolutionary strategy for many tropical bamboos, and may also contribute to the evolutionary pressure maintaining synchrony among the species important to the pandas as food, other factors probably also play a part. Even among the giant bamboo species it has been noticed that insect pests of shoots and stems increase at flowering time. (Brazilian folk-lore has it that the plagues of rats which follow the flowering of the indigenous bamboo species hatch from grubs that grow in the base of the stems (Derby, 1879).) Shoots of the umbrella bamboo are often destroyed by the larvae of anthomyiid flies, a group which includes common plant-boring pests like the cabbage root fly and wheat bulb fly, and by beetle larvae, both of which feed on the fleshy interior of the bamboo shoots. In the early 1980s at Wolong, some areas of *Fargesia* were losing so many shoots each year that too few were surviving to replace the old stems as they died. While it might be tempting to conclude from this that the starvation and death of animals feeding on shoots is more important than the control of seed predators, there are other possible explanations. In particular, the eradication of bamboo at low altitudes resulting from an expansion of farming in the valleys and the flowering of arrow bamboo higher up the mountain had concentrated many bamboo predators into a smaller area, and this may account for the high levels of predation on *Fargesia* shoots in Wolong.

No study has yet succeeded in untangling the complex web of cause and effect to decide whether it is the control of shoot predators or seed predators that is most important for the long-term survival of plants like the umbrella and arrow bamboos. With the limited, largely anecdotal information available at the moment, the answer must await further research. Many of the reported explosions in the populations of rats and mice are probably the result of shoot-eaters migrating from areas where bamboo has died, and moving onto agricultural land where they do enough damage to gain attention. To the farmer, it appears that numbers have increased to plague proportions, but the truth may be that the population is the same as it ever was, or even that many animals have died of starvation before migrating.

The strategy of synchronous flowering may also help the bamboo in other ways. By suppressing the production of seed when conditions are favourable, the plants can invest more energy in vegetative growth. Spreading across the forest floor and growing above other herbs and grasses, the bamboos compete very effectively with plants that have adopted other, more orthodox, lifestyles. If, as suggested above, flowering is correlated with periods of drought, synchrony may also help the bamboo to survive in a variable climate. Bamboos generally occur only in areas where rainfall and humidity are high. Ample water is particularly important for shoot production, and in times of drought a plant's best strategy may well be to set seed and die, rather than to produce a few, slow-growing shoots that would most likely become food for the now hungry shoot-eaters. Seedlings need less water and will survive the shoot-predators, so by concentrating its energies on seed production, the bamboo solves both its problems elegantly.

The genetic mechanism that underlies synchronous flowering is still a mystery, and all speculations on how this mechanism interacts with the climate are tentative. However, it is clear that once the system is established, synchronous flowering will be maintained by the very animals it keeps under control. Plants that flower early or late in the cycle will lose far more of their seeds than those that flower in phase with the majority and drop their seeds into a world of overstuffed seed-eaters. Plants that remain alive after others in the neighbourhood have flowered will be heavily grazed by herbivores, especially bamboo specialists like the pandas, and their flowers and shoots will be attacked remorselessly by all those flies and beetles that are looking for somewhere to lay their eggs.

The mechanisms underlying the control of bamboo flowering outlined above are still far from proven, and the suggestion that earthquakes may be involved is extremely controversial, but a complex interaction between a genetically programmed flowering period and a drought-induced stimulation of flowering would go a long way towards explaining how different species growing in the same area manage to synchronise their flowering periods. In the eastern Min mountains, three different species, *Fargesia scabrida*, *F. robusta* and *F. nitida* all flowered simultaneously between 1974 and 1976. Such 'sympatric' flowering has been recorded repeatedly, though how much the coincidence of flowering is the result of chance or of human intervention rather than evolution and drought is a matter of some doubt.

Once the bamboo has flowered, the re-establishment of a crop capable of supporting bamboo specialists like the panda is a very, very slow process. Seeds of the arrow bamboo *Gelidocalamus fangianus* remain dormant in the soil for at least two years, and seeds of *F. scabrida* remained in the soil and did not begin to germinate until five years after this species flowered throughout the Min mountains in 1975 and 1976. Once they have germinated, the new seedlings of both species grow slowly, taking 15 years or more to reach maturity (Taylor and Qin, 1988a).

The periodic flowering and death of the bamboo under-storey is essential to maintain the vigour of the bamboo, and on a larger scale it also determines the nature of the forest itself. Where bamboo grows densely, it intercepts what little sunlight penetrates beneath the massive firs and hemlocks. Only when the bamboo under-storey has died after flowering can light reach the seedlings of these great trees. A mass die-off also releases nutrients which can act as fertiliser for the growing saplings. Where there is a dense stand of bamboo, few tree seedlings become established during the years between flowering events. In some patches of uncut forest in the Wolong Reserve, where there is a dense under-storey of arrow bamboo, there are many 95-year-old trees. Their establishment as seedlings would have occurred at the same time as the die-off of arrow bamboo following the flowering in 1893.

Though not obvious at first glance, there are areas where the forest has the look of a plantation, with all trees at almost exactly the same age. Just at the moment, there are a lot of seedlings, but the establishment of new trees does not always coincide with flowering events. The arrow bamboo at Wolong flowered again in 1935, but there is no corresponding generation of 50-year-old trees. Throughout the last century it seems that small-scale disturbances like landslips and tree-falls have been more important in releasing light and nutrients and allowing tree seedlings to become established than the mass-flowering event of 55 years ago (Taylor and Qin, 1989).

By cutting out the light that reaches the forest floor and locking up the available nutrients, a dense bamboo under-storey can make it almost impossible for tree seedlings to grow. Before the bamboo flowers, the few saplings in the forest tend to be on raised surfaces like fallen logs, or close to trails where there is more light. Many older trees have weirdly-bent trunks, evidence that their early years were spent growing atop a fallen log. Birches are particularly adept at establishing themselves in this way, and where the bamboo grows most densely they may outnumber the firs (Taylor and Qin, 1988a).

Just as bamboos affect the growth of trees, so the trees influence the growth of bamboo. Some bamboos quickly invade cleared ground, but many species that are important to the pandas provide suitable forage only when growing beneath trees. When an area is clear felled, arrow bamboo grows densely at first—so densely that it becomes almost impenetrable even to giant pandas. But the seedlings of arrow bamboo are thin and shallow rooted, and are easily killed by drought or overrun by more robust plants. In areas where the forest has been felled, few seedlings survive. Beneath the shade of the canopy on the other hand, where evaporation is slow and competing grasses cannot grow, the ground is soon covered with delicate green leaves, the next generation of arrow bamboo. Similarly, the stone bamboo *Yushania chungii* cannot re-establish itself after flowering in cleared forest, and is soon replaced by drought-tolerant grasses and a scrub of currant and rose bushes (Ma, 1985).

To manipulate such a complex ecosystem in an attempt to help conserve the pandas could be dangerous. It is now obvious from the understanding gained over the last ten years that the once popular idea of introducing other bamboo species as an alternative food source for pandas when the endemic species flower could upset what may be a delicate balance between forest cover and bamboo flowering cycles. It is human destruction of its habitat that threatens the survival of the panda in the wild and not the bamboo's peculiar habit of flowering and dying. Bamboo has been flowering periodically for millions of years, but until the latest flowering episode there have been no records of pandas dying as a consequence. Until recently the pandas in these mountains had a wider variety of potential foods, including the subtropical species that were once widespread in the valley bottoms. These low altitude species would in previous times have sustained the panda population, excepting those animals too old or sick to cope with the stress of moving or changing diet. Perhaps even more important to pandas in the past were the semi-tropical *Phyllostachys* species. There are some 50 species in this genus, and most are difficult to distinguish although the black-stemmed Whangee cane (*Phyllostachys nigra*) is distinctive, and widely cultivated in the West. *Phyllostachys* species often have very long periods between flowerings, and are apparently less susceptible to environmental influences than the temperate species. These semi-tropical species are perfectly acceptable to the pandas as food, and in the Foping

Reserve in southern Shaanxi, *Phyllostachys* is still an important part of the giant pandas' diet. In the Wolong Reserve the pandas probably never move below 1,600 m, and into the few remaining patches of subtropical broad-leaved forest. In other reserves where this evergreen forest with its tanbark oak and camphor trees is more widespread and where there is less human interference, they have been reported as low as 800 m (Campbell and Qin, 1983).

Unfortunately, throughout much of the panda's range, most of the deciduous forest in which these low-altitude bamboos once flourished has now been felled, and the valley floor and lower slopes have been cleared for agriculture. In the Baishuijiang reserve in southern Gansu province, for example, the bamboo growing beneath the broad-leaved forest (*Yushania chungii*) has been severely depleted, and when the higher-altitude species flowered and died in 1975, a third of the pandas could find no alternative source of food and died of starvation (Ma, 1985). Where isolated patches of low-altitude bamboo remain, pandas often avoid moving close to villages to feed on them, although the pandas at Baishuijiang were quite often seen within 50 m of a house and would raid fields for wheat, corn and buckwheat.

There is no doubt that it is the destruction of valley habitat for farming and the consequent elimination of these low-altitude bamboos that has been responsible for the starvation and death of giant pandas during the latest burst of flowering. With no food at all, the pandas could only migrate or die. In the Wanglang reserve where *Fargesia nitida* is the only significant source of food for pandas, a population of 196 animals was reduced to between 10 and 20 in less than three years. Between 1974 and 1977 a total of 138 pandas were found dead in the eastern Min mountains, and doubtless many more deaths went undiscovered (Mackinnon, 1986).

The bamboo die-off in Wanglang Reserve was almost complete, but fortunately for the animals flowering is often patchy, and spread over several years. In the Qionglai mountains, flowering of arrow bamboo reached a peak in 1983. Sixty-two dead pandas were found, 25 captured and moved to areas with bamboo, and 47 'rescued' and taken into captivity, where 18 died later of starvation (Schaller, 1988). Yet in the Wolong Reserve, in the heart of the present burst of flowering, only about 82 per cent of the arrow bamboo has flowered. One subadult panda emigrated, and two that were in poor health and old may have had their demise hastened by the food shortage, but no animals starved. Flowering has not significantly affected the reproductive rate of the remaining animals.

In some cases the islands of vegetation that are left after a major flowering may be able to support pandas and other bamboo eaters until seedlings have grown large enough to provide an adequate food source. If the islands are too small, the animals must either feed on other bamboo species, or migrate to areas where the bamboo is not flowering. In cultivation, with the help of fertilisers, some bamboo species can be encouraged to regenerate from the rhizomes of the parent plant, but I know of no evidence that this happens in panda country, where the soil is generally poor.

Don Reid, a biologist working on the joint China/WWF Panda

Research Project, worked for three years in Wolong after the flowering of arrow bamboo. Much of this time he spent climbing the steep slopes, painstakingly mapping almost three quarters of the forest under-storey in a 25 km² study area. As a result of this almost superhuman effort, fuelled by legendary quantities of rice and noodles, we now have a clear idea of how the pandas in Wolong managed to survive the flowering of arrow bamboo with so few deaths. His study confirms that the survival of umbrella bamboo at low altitudes has been crucial in preventing the starvation of pandas. Three years after flowering, leaves of umbrella bamboo became the most important component of the giant panda's diet during January and February (Reid *et al.*, 1989).

When no alternative foods are available, pandas are forced to migrate, which it seems they are extremely reluctant to do. They are in fact deeply conservative animals, and do not readily change the habits of a lifetime. Their biology demands that they have an intimate knowledge of their home range, so that they can move about within it efficiently, never far from water, never having to climb steep ridges when there is a level trail that will take them to the same spot. Only three radio-collared animals have ever been released successfully into the wild from captivity, and two of these returned to take up residence in or very close to their original ranges. Nothing but the threat of starvation will force an animal to abandon the hills and valleys it is familiar with and move into unknown terrain. Paradoxically, the periodic flowering and death of bamboo may be essential to the survival of the pandas, simply because it forces them to move.

In spring, as the breeding season approaches, males use their intimate knowledge of the terrain and of the other animals in the area to locate potential mates (see p. 83 *et seq.*). Groups of animals are often effectively isolated from each other by high ridges, river valleys, and increasingly by tracts of agricultural land or cleared forest. High ridges are not insurmountable barriers to panda movements, and panda droppings have been found 300 m above the rhododendron forests and 450 m above the nearest bamboo, confirming that they will on occasion venture a considerable distance from their normal habitat (Sheldon, 1937). Pandas are also perfectly capable of crossing small rivers, but no panda will venture out of the area it knows well at a time when reproductive success depends largely on an intimate knowledge of the terrain and of the other animals within its range. Even before the appearance of man-made barriers, pandas within each drainage basin might well have become inbred, were it not for the occasional upheaval caused by the bamboo die-off.

Once a new generation of seedlings has re-established the bamboo under-storey, pandas have a very easy time of it. After the first few months of life they have few enemies, and there is little competition between animals other than between males for access to females at mating time. Under these conditions animals with mutations and gene combinations that might be lethal in more stressful times, can survive and breed. Because the population is small and inbreeding, the number of animals carrying these inherited traits can increase, while the genes for more useful characteristics are lost, a process known to biologists as 'genetic drift'. Just how important the flowering of the bamboo and the consequent forced migrations are in preventing inbreeding and genetic drift is still a matter for speculation, since little is known about the genetics of the wild panda population (see pp. 119–25). But it is certainly clear that the panda is much better adapted to its capricious environment than anyone suspected back in 1980.

Bamboo flowering creates a similar set of problems for red pandas. Their more varied diet might be expected to make life easier for them when the bamboo flowers, but there is little evidence to suggest that red pandas change their feeding habits at all. Berries and birds eggs may be important in their season, but do not provide a year-round substitute for bamboo, and since the red panda is not a specialised hunter it cannot hope to survive on birds and small mammals alone. But in coping with the crisis of flowering, red pandas have several advantages. Because they do not sit in order to feed, they can forage on steeper slopes than those favoured by giant pandas. They can also feed efficiently on the shorter-growing bamboo at altitudes above the giant panda's normal range. However, it may be that other factors outweigh these advantages and make bamboo flowering even more threatening for red pandas than it is for giant pandas. In particular, red pandas do not leave their normal range to forage on different bamboo species as the seasons change. If red pandas cannot move easily when the bamboo within their home range flowers, either because of aggression from neighbours or because an intimate knowledge of their home range is important for day-to-day survival, then flowering may be a disaster. All that is certain is that red pandas have survived many previous bamboo-flowering events. If previous generations of red pandas have survived without migrating, or moved to higher altitudes, then the present generation will not be as badly effected by the habitat destruction in the lowlands as the giant pandas.

Unfortunately, all this is speculation. Red pandas have hardly been studied at all in the wild, and although there are no reports of red panda deaths following bamboo flowering, this could be either because they are small and difficult to find when dead, or because deaths were not considered important enough to report.

Notes

1. At least there are no records of *Ailurus* in the extensive list of Pleistocene cave fauna from south China given by *Kahlke, Vertebrata Palasiatica*, vol. 2 (1961), pp. 83–108.
2. The taxonomy of bamboos in Nepal is even more confused than in China, and no attempt has been made to allocate scientific names to these species.

3. The Solitary Panda

The great French zoologist Cuvier, who first gave the red panda its scientific name, is once supposed to have bragged 'show me a claw, and I will show you the whole structure of the animal that bore it.' A detailed study of an animal's anatomy does indeed provide much information about its natural history, although the curved and semi-retractile claws of the red panda are not so different from those of a cat or marten. For the early zoologists who pored over skeletons of the giant and red pandas, it was the teeth that provided the first clues that they were dealing with very unusual beasts.

On each side of both the upper and lower jaws, the red panda has three incisors and two canines. In the upper jaw there are three premolars on each side, and in the lower jaw there are four. Behind these there are two molars. This 'dental formula' is typical of carnivores, except that the fourth upper premolar is missing. But the teeth themselves are far from typical. Most carnivores have the last premolar in the upper jaw and the first molar in the lower jaw modified to act as scissors, with sharp tips, high cusps and jagged edges that fit together perfectly for shearing meat into easily swallowed pieces. The cheek teeth of the red panda on the other hand are all unusually large, flat and broad with a complex pattern of ridges. The giant panda is similarly equipped but with four premolars and two molars in the upper jaw, and four (sometimes three) premolars and three molars in the lower. Again, the posterior premolars and molars are broad, flat and heavily ridged.

The bears have similarly lost the typical meat-slicing teeth, in response to their largely vegetarian diet. Apart from the polar bear, which has a purely carnivorous diet (and may be in the process of evolving flesh-shearing teeth again), most bears rely on plant matter for over 75 per cent of their food. Much the same pattern is found in the racoons, and only the cacomistle from Central America has retained the flesh-cutting teeth typical of carnivores. But in neither family has any other animal taken the process of specialisation as far as the red and giant pandas. In both pandas the teeth are in many ways more like those of a ruminant herbivore than a carnivore. Both also have unusually heavily boned skulls for their size, and the deep skull and prominent cheekbones provide strong anchor points for the powerful muscles that close the jaws. All these developments can be explained as a series of subtle adaptations to the pandas' uniquely specialised diet of bamboo.

The diet of both red and giant pandas is made up almost exclusively of bamboo, which is remarkable because the gut of a panda is not adapted to break down most of the chemically complex fibrous materials that account for the bulk of its chosen food. Most herbivores have evolved some means of digesting the energy-rich cellulose that constitutes the structural material of plant-cell walls. The ruminants (cattle, sheep, antelope, goats and deer) have a modified stomach where food is fermented by bacteria. In the rumen these bacteria break down cellulose to simple sugars before the food is regurgitated and chewed a second time. The cud is then passed back to a second chamber where the normal process of digestion and absorption begins. In non-ruminant herbivores, like the rabbit, elephant and rhinoceros, food is partially digested in the stomach and small intestine before

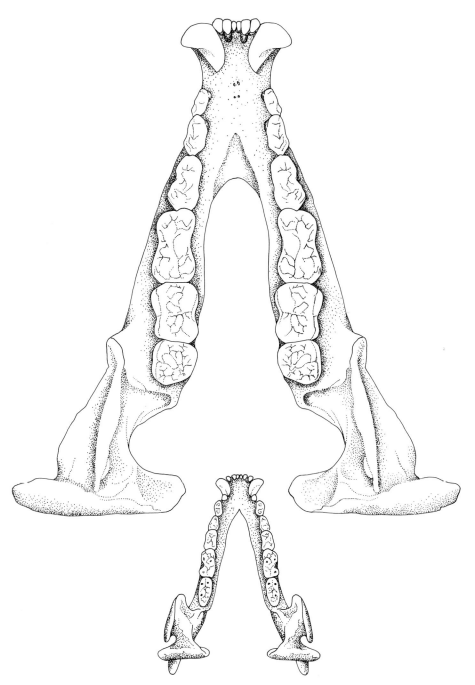

Figure 7. The lower jaw of a giant panda (above) and a red panda (below). In both, the cheek teeth are broad and heavily ridged, ideal for grinding bamboo.

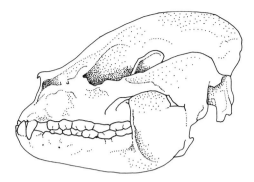

Figure 8. Skull of a giant panda (left) and red panda (right). The heavy bone structure provides articulation for the muscles needed to chew through their tough diet.

being passed into a blind sac called the caecum, where once again bacteria help dismantle the long cellulose fibres.

Neither red nor giant pandas have any such specialisation of the digestive system. The intestine of a giant panda is a little over four times the length of its body (Liu, 1984), no longer than that of a meat-eating bear of the same size. The intestine of the red panda is between four and five times the length of its body, similar to that of a carnivorous racoon or civet. In neither are there micro-organisms in the gut to help break down the indigestible cell walls. While this is unusual among herbivores, it is not unique. The howler monkeys of South America are leaf-eaters that like the pandas have only taken up this specialised diet recently in their evolutionary history. Although howler monkeys do have a caecum that is capable of limited fermentation, it is nowhere near as developed as the same organ in old-world specialist leaf-eaters like the proboscis or colobus monkeys. Howler monkeys, like pandas, must choose their food carefully if they are to get enough energy from it to keep themselves alive and not fill their stomachs with indigestible roughage. To a lesser extent, this is also true of many other leaf-eating monkeys and apes—gorillas, orangutans, siamangs, and some lemurs too have only limited digestive specialisations to their diet (Milton, 1978).

The gut of the giant panda does make a few concessions to the formidable challenge posed by its diet. The wall of the oesophagus is tough and horny, and the stomach is thick-walled and muscular. These developments are absent from the same organs in the red panda. The giant panda, with its habit of eating quantities of bamboo stem, is obviously more in need of protection against sharp bamboo splinters than the red panda, whose diet consists almost exclusively of leaves and shoots.

While bamboo accounts for some 99 per cent of the diet of giant pandas, the red panda is slightly less of a specialist. For many years the only information on their diet came from B. H. Hodgson, who studied their habits in captivity in northern India. He kept several animals as pets for over a year, and reported that they fed happily on fruits, tuberous roots, acorns, beech mast, eggs and bamboo shoots, but that

> In general the wahs [red pandas] eschew flesh, fish, insects, reptiles, absolutely. But they love milk and ghee, and constantly make their way furtively into remote dairies and cowherds' cottages to possess themselves of these luxuries. (Hodgson, 1847)

Hodgson offered his animals rats, fish, insects and snakes which they always refused, presumably because the animals were dead and red pandas rarely scavenge carrion. Live chickens were occasionally killed but never eaten, but we now know that red pandas do indeed stalk, kill and eat animals. Captive animals in Washington Zoo repeatedly tried to catch birds, and sometimes succeeded (Roberts, 1982), and captives at the Cotswold Wildlife Park in England catch and eat small rabbits, rats and birds (S. Blackwell, pers. comm. 1982). This carnivorous behaviour is particularly noticeable in pregnant females (Bleijenberg, 1984). In the wild the animals in Wolong take fruit when it is available. *Sorbus* and *Ribes* berries are eaten in autumn, and red pandas probably eat birds eggs whenever they find them, but bamboo still accounts for some 95 per cent of their food. In Nepal fruits and berries make up a larger proportion of the animals' diet. In the Langtang National Park the leaves and shoots of jhapra bamboo meet more than 80 per cent of the red pandas' dietary needs, but they also move up and down the mountains to take advantage of seasonal crops of *Sorbus cuspidata* and *S. microphylla* berries which together account for over 15 per cent of their food annually. Raate bamboo is only occasionally eaten, and the only other food items found in faeces were mushrooms, which account for less than 2 per cent of the animals' dietary intake (Yonzon and Hunter, 1989).

Apparently, the first person to record the importance of bamboo in the diet of red pandas was Floyd Tangier Smith.

> From the report of natives in places where they occur it seems pretty certain that the lesser panda also eats a good deal of tree moss, and it is certain that the few that have been kept in captivity will eat, and can thrive on, corn and several other herbs and vegetables. But it is equally certain that he is a strict vegetarian, and that, in the wild state, the bamboo leaf is his bread and butter, and his first choice at meal time wherever he may be. (Smith, 1932)

In Wolong red pandas feed almost exclusively on the leaves of arrow bamboo, with shoots making up only about 5 per cent of their diet. Each winter about a third of the leaves on a bamboo stem die, and red pandas avoid these, nipping off only the freshest and most nutritious. Carefully taking one at a time, almost all the selected leaves are bitten off exactly where the leaf joins the branch. Captive animals introduced to growing bamboo will either sit or stand on their hind legs, using their paws to grasp a stem and bend it over so that they can reach the leaves growing at the tip. Leaves close to the ground are simply bitten off. All leaves are chewed very thoroughly, presumably enabling the animal to digest more of the cell contents than is possible for the giant panda (Johnson *et al.*, 1988).

A giant panda, with its habit of holding bunches of leaves in one paw and biting through the whole mass at once, cannot be a fastidious feeder. Instead of selecting the titbits from a stand of bamboo, the giant panda goes for bulk processing. A giant panda feeding on leaves will chew them fairly carefully, but stem is chewed only briefly. Differences between the red and giant pandas' attitudes to their diet are obvious from even a cursory study of their droppings. Giant panda droppings are a mass of bamboo splinters, so poorly chewed that the length of splinters gives a good idea of the 'bite size' and hence the age of the animal responsible. Red panda droppings are a mass of finely pulverised plant tissue.

Following the tracks of giant pandas can give some idea of their foraging behaviour. In April 1987, after a night of heavy snow, I tracked an unknown adult across a steep hillside in Wolong. At an altitude of about 2,700 m, the trail followed a contour separating the shorter, slender arrow bamboo growing up the slope from the taller, denser umbrella bamboo which predominates in the valleys. About 100 m from where I joined the tracks, the animal ate three or four stems of arrow bamboo. Panda tracks are usually difficult to follow and interpret, but here the discarded tops of bamboo lying on the fresh-fallen snow, and the marks where the animal sat to feed, propped against a low bank, wrote an unmistakable story. Close by was a single dropping, at the base of a spindly maple. Five metres further on a single stem had been bitten off, and a few metres beyond this, another. At this point there was bamboo all around the trail, but the panda kept to the easy, horizontal track, rather than move up or down the slope to feed. A few metres beyond, it climbed a bank, and headed into a patch of thicker bamboo. Here half-eaten stems lay everywhere, and tracks began to criss-cross each other, showing where the animal had wandered, apparently at random, through the bamboo. Beneath a massive fir tree lay a pile of 18 droppings, frozen hard, and scattered all around were bamboo leaves and bits of stem. Compacted snow beneath the tree marked where the animal sat to rest.

In many ways this is typical feeding behaviour. In Wolong giant pandas spend almost all their time in arrow bamboo, and descend to umbrella bamboo only for a short period in May and June, when they feed on the soft, fleshy shoots. Often an animal will eat most of the stems in one area, then move on through what to human eyes is a mass of identical plants. George Schaller tracked a subadult that ate only occasionally until entering a patch of tall but sparse bamboo where it 'consumed 78 stems in 13 m before resuming its intermittent foraging' (Schaller *et al.*, 1985). Once settled in a comfortable spot, an animal will sometimes eat everything within reach. What makes one piece of bamboo more attractive to a panda than another is a mystery. Captive animals sniff the stems of bamboo before beginning to feed, but what information this reveals can only be guessed at.

Typical too is the way in which only part of a stem was eaten and the rest discarded. Although there are leaves on the bamboo throughout the year, giant pandas avoid eating leaves between March and June, concentrating throughout this period on stems and new shoots. During this brief period the old shoots contain higher levels of essential amino acids than do leaves, but this cannot be the whole story. The leaves of umbrella bamboo contain more essential amino acids than the shoots all year round, but animals also avoid eating leaves of umbrella bamboo during spring. Overall, arrow bamboo contains more protein and digestible carbohydrate than umbrella bamboo, which may influence an animal's choice of food, but probably more important than this is the difficulty of feeding on umbrella bamboo. Umbrella bamboo is exhausting for humans to move through, and the same may well be true for pandas, even though their squat, roly-poly shape is far

8. Even when moving across patchy snow, the giant panda's markings provide little by way of camouflage. *(Zig Leczczynski/Animals Animals/Oxford Scientific Films)*

9. Red panda sunbathing in the Wolong reserve. Behind, Mt Siguniang rises to over 6000m. *(Lao Er Pen)*

10. By carefully nipping off individual leaves, red pandas avoid filling their stomach with indigestible bulk. *(Chris Catton)*

Figure 9. By sitting down to feed, giant pandas save precious energy. It is for this reason that they avoid steep slopes where it would be impossible to eat in comfort.

better suited to the task than the cumbersome human frame. The stems are thick, close growing and tangled. Umbrella bamboo also takes longer to eat. Giant pandas can eat arrow bamboo just by holding a stem in one paw and biting bits from the end. Umbrella bamboo is sometimes peeled before it is eaten, the stem covering and sheaths stripped away with the teeth to expose the central core which is then bitten off like celery. This may save the animal from carrying indigestible bulk in i stomach, but it takes time, and pandas have little time to spare.

Umbrella bamboo grows at a lower altitude, often covering the steep slopes above rivers and gullies, and tracks show that pandas almost always walk along a contour rather than climb up or down a steep bank, so saving energy. Analysis of the giant pandas' diet shows that they obtain more than enough protein from the bamboo they eat. Getting enough energy is their main problem. George Schaller calculates that in spring, when arrow bamboo stems are the main source of food, an animal would take 19.4 hours to eat the 12.5 kg of bamboo it needs just to keep going (Schaller *et al.*, 1985). The lack of any gut micro-organisms means that while subsisting on this relatively poor fodder, an animal can probably only digest about 12 per cent of the food it eats. Animals are active on average for only 15.4 hours a day in spring, so either the calculations are wrong, or the animal is actually losing weight through this lean period of the year. Whichever of these alternatives turns out to be correct, it is obvious that pandas must forage efficiently if they are to survive. Even in summer, when food supply is at its most nutritious, pandas can lay down only a little fat. It is probably for this reason, and because it has a constant supply of food, that unlike most bears the giant panda does not hibernate.

The general pattern at Wolong is that an animal spends from July to October feeding mostly on the leaves of arrow bamboo, with stem becoming increasingly important in the diet through winter, until in spring the emphasis shifts to umbrella bamboo shoots. These shoots are wrapped in tough, hairy sheaths which the animal must first remove, a fiddly operation even for humans. I found it difficult to strip the sheaths from a shoot without breaking the shoot itself. A panda simply holds the shoot in one paw and strips it with its teeth, dropping the sheath onto its lap or between its legs in one fluid, dexterous movement. But even for pandas who are masters at the art of shoot-stripping, it is slow work. In an effort to get as many calories into themselves as possible, pandas concentrate on eating thick shoots, and rarely enter a patch of bamboo to feed, preferring to forage around the edge where it is easier to move, and where the density of shoots is highest. In this way, an adult panda may eat some 650 shoots in a day, weighing a total of 38 kg or a quarter of its body weight (Schaller, 1986). Pandas feeding on the heavier shoots of *Phyllostachys* in the Qinling mountains are reported to consume even more, possibly as much as 57 kg a day (Yong, 1981).

Why do giant pandas in Wolong eat umbrella bamboo shoots in spring? Bamboo shoots are 90 per cent water, and while feeding on them the panda does not need to drink. For the rest of the year pandas must drink once a day, usually from one of the many small rivulets that trickle down the mountainsides. Yet the constant presence of water makes it very unlikely that this is the reason for the change of diet, especially since spring is almost the wettest time of year. Pandas probably have more trouble finding water in winter, when creeks are frozen hard, and when to eat snow would be energetically costly because of the heat that would be lost in melting it. Perhaps more significant is that most umbrella bamboo shoots emerge when the nutritional quality of arrow bamboo leaves and stems is low. New shoots are rich in protein and carbohydrate, and contain fairly high levels of essential amino acids (Schaller *et al.*, 1985).

While most animals follow this annual feeding cycle, individuals may have rather different habits. One collared male spent much of his time feeding in umbrella bamboo all year, while in 1987 an adult female spent most of April feeding in umbrella bamboo on stems and leaves, ignoring large stands of arrow bamboo on easy terrain only 30 m above her. Young animals sometimes do not descend in spring to feed on bamboo shoots, but remain in the arrow bamboo eating old stems. Outside the well-studied Wolong Reserve, the picture becomes even more complex. Different species of bamboo grow in different mountain systems, and so areas may vary both in the type and number of bamboo species available to pandas as food. In the Min mountains, some 150 km to the north of Wolong, arrow bamboo (*Gelidocalamus fangianus*) rarely grows at high altitude, and is replaced in some areas by sword bamboo (*Fargesia nitida*), and in others by *F. denudata*. Possibly periods of warm, dry climate during the Tertiary era eliminated the arrow bamboo from these mountains, allowing the other species to replace it when the present cooler and wetter conditions returned. In the Tangjiahe Reserve, *F. scabrida* is the main bamboo species between 1,600 m and 2,300 m and has been the primary source of food for giant pandas since *F. denudata* flowered extensively above 2,300 m in the mid-1970s. Pandas feed on leaves from October to March, and on leaves and stems from March to June. The shoots of *F. scabrida* grow between August and September, when they become the main source of food (Taylor and Qin, 1987; Schaller *et al.*, 1989). In the Qinling mountains of southern Shaanxi province, *F. aurita* was the most important food for pandas until the plant flowered and died in the 1970s. A study carried out between 1980 and 1981 (Young, 1981), shortly after the flowering, found that the pandas were feeding instead on a species named in the report as *Phyllostachys* but which in fact was probably *Bashania fargesii* (Wu, 1986). From March through to mid April pandas ate leaves and 1 to 2-year-old stem, changing to feeding on shoots during the summer. With the coming of autumn, the pandas switch again to feeding mostly on leaves. In the Baishuijiang Reserve in southern Gansu province, a *Fargesia* species growing between 2,000 and 3,100 m is the preferred panda food, but following the die-off in 1975 the pandas moved to lower altitudes to feed on stone bamboo (*Yushania chungii*).

In the south of the panda's range the dominant bamboos are different again. At lower altitudes the bamboos are more closely related to the tropical and subtropical species than to the temperate species of the north. In the Liang mountain system pandas feed on *Chimonobambusa szechuanensis*, *Qiongzhuea tumidiroda*, *Q. opienensis*, *Indocalamus longiauritus* and *Yushania chungii*. However, due to the encroachment of agriculture on the lower slopes they are generally forced to remain high on the mountains, concentrating their feeding on *G. fangianus* and *F. nitida* (Hu, 1985). In all, giant pandas are known to feed on at least 30 different species of bamboo belonging to nine genera. Yet in spite of the variable conditions and the range of species that provide food for pandas, a migration to lower altitudes to feed on thick shoots in spring does seem to be consistent.

Why has the giant panda become so specialised in feeding on bamboo? Pandas are quite capable of eating other plants, and after the bamboo die-off in the Min mountains, pandas are known to have eaten shrubs, the bark of trees and a variety of herbs. One captive animal released into a large enclosure during our stay in Wolong on a warm afternoon in late April began feeding on fresh grass, bending forward and biting off mouthfuls which it then chewed briefly. Seeds of mature grasses are occasionally found in the droppings of wild animals, and there are several reports of animals eating grass in times of severe bamboo shortage.

Giant pandas will also eat meat. In Wanglang villagers found the remains of small rodents in the stomachs of wild pandas (Giant Panda Expedition, 1974), and Schaller found hair, bones and hooves of musk deer in the droppings of one animal, and hair of golden monkey in another. One night we inadvertently left a small quantity of meat in a tent pitched on a high ridge, and returned the next day to find several neat claw-marks in the fabric, and the tent totally flattened where the animal had rolled on it—I imagine in frustration. The panda research project has successfully used meat to lure pandas into traps, smoking it first on a small bonfire to fill the air with scent. I watched another captive animal at the breeding centre in Wolong eat the hind leg of a fully grown pig, biting through the femur as if it were a stick of seaside rock, which perhaps gives some idea of the power in those immense jaws. And yet pandas eat little meat, almost certainly because they rarely get the luxury of choice.

Although there is a wide variety of potential food in these mountains for a large carnivore—wolves and leopards survive despite persecution—the prey is scattered over a wide area, never at very high density. There are few opportunities for scavenging, and the giant panda's clumsy gait hardly seems ideally suited to running down a musk deer or serow, although a panda can move with remarkable speed if given a good enough reason. Instead, the giant panda has taken another path, choosing to feed on a poor but plentiful diet. On this diet the giant panda grows slowly to reach its adult weight (80–125 kg for wild-caught animals) in approximately three years. Adults vary considerably in size, but males are on average slightly heavier than females.

Apart from the shoot-predators (see Chapter 2) few animals compete with the pandas for food. Takin eat bamboo leaves, and occasionally so may golden monkeys and deer. Local people in panda country use stems to weave baskets and to make other household goods, but compared with the indirect impact of logging and agriculture the effect of this is insignificant. Apart from the red panda, there is only one other animal in the giant panda's habitat that lives exclusively on bamboo; the bamboo rat, *Rhizomys sinense*.

Bamboo rats spend almost all their lives underground, in a network of tunnels that may cover an area of over 200 m². The adults weigh about 1 kg and are about 40 cm long, covered in a soft coat of thick, grey fur. Their eyes are small, and their short legs are well adapted for digging in the stony mountain soil. Their tails are short, and so with the exception of the vicious looking incisors they have the appearance of a cuddly bundle of fur. The young are particularly attractive and would make good pets were it not for the vast quantity of bamboo they eat, and the fact that they grow up into adults with teeth like wire-cutters.

Bamboo rats have two methods of feeding. From beneath the ground, they cut neatly through a bamboo stem and drag the aerial portion down into the burrow where it can be eaten safely. Alternatively, they emerge at night to bite through stems above the ground, then pull the severed stem back into the burrow which they close behind them with earth and stones. Often, only part of a stem is eaten, and the bits of dying bamboo stem poking at peculiar angles from disturbed earth are the easily identified signs of a bamboo rat's burrow.

In the Wolong Reserve bamboo rats are reasonably common. In early May, with the help of local researchers, we caught a mother and her three

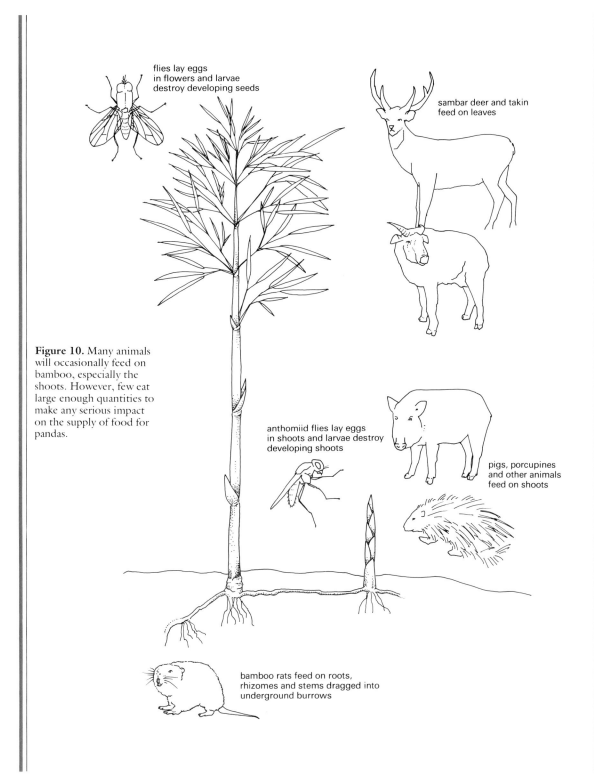

flies lay eggs
in flowers and larvae
destroy developing seeds

sambar deer and takin
feed on leaves

Figure 10. Many animals
will occasionally feed on
bamboo, especially the
shoots. However, few eat
large enough quantities to
make any serious impact
on the supply of food for
pandas.

anthomiid flies lay eggs
in shoots and larvae destroy
developing shoots

pigs, porcupines
and other animals
feed on shoots

bamboo rats feed on roots,
rhizomes and stems dragged into
underground burrows

young and kept them in captivity for several days in order to film their behaviour. The young were already weaned, and like their mother were feeding on stems and branches of bamboo, obviously preferring the thin, one-year-old stems to both shoots and older, tougher stems. When feeding, the young would pull bamboo through the roof of their artificial tunnel holding the stem in their teeth. Then they would lie on their sides or backs, usually with their eyes closed, and feed the tip of the stem into their mouths with their front legs, nibbling away frantically. Their droppings, which are usually deposited in special latrine sites, show that the food is chewed to the consistency of fine sawdust. Even the leaves were eaten, and only the sheaths around the stems were discarded. In this manner the family chewed their way through a considerable quantity of bamboo, day and night. In the wild the mother and young had apparently spent much of their time in a nest chamber a metre below the surface and about 50 cm in diameter, the floor of which was covered with a litter of bamboo leaves, tissue stripped from the outside of stems, and some branches. According to local hunters, males live in separate burrow systems, and their nests contain only torn stems and no leaves.

For all their activity, it is unlikely that bamboo rats make much impact on the panda's food supply. Although the rats are not uncommon, there are few sites where the soil is deep enough to allow the construction of their elaborate network of burrows. They are scattered, and their numbers are probably kept in check by stoats and weasels. By thinning out dense stands of bamboo it is even possible that the rats encourage shoot production, which would subsequently benefit pandas.

Avoiding unnecessary energy expenditure, and feeding steadily through-out the day and night, the panda survives with an almost robotic efficiency. When not eating or travelling, it sleeps, curled up in a bamboo patch, often with its head resting on a hind leg as a pillow, or propped against the base of a large fir or hemlock tree where the collected needles make a dry and pre-sumably comfortable bed, insulated a little from the cold soil beneath. Sometimes an animal will seek out a hollow tree or cave in which to shelter, especially in heavy, continuous rain. Indeed, it seems that this is exactly what the panda shot by Theodore and Kermit Roosevelt was doing just before it died. After a night of snow and a morning of thin misty rain, the Roosevelts tracked down a panda in the mountains south-west of Chengdu.

Figure 11. Red and giant pandas sleeping. The diet of red and giant pandas forces both animals to save energy whenever possible. When sleeping, the red panda avoids losing heat to the atmosphere by wrapping its extremities in its thick tail. It also avoids losing heat to the often frozen ground by sleeping in the fork of a tree. Giant pandas can achieve the same result by selecting areas thick in pine needles as resting sites, and by sleeping with their head propped on a hind leg.

Their guide, Mokhta Lone, left the trail to investigate a sound and then motioned for Kermit to join him.

> As I gained his side, he pointed to a giant spruce tree thirty yards away. The bole was hollowed, and from it emerged the head and forequarters of a beishung. He looked sleepily from side to side as he sauntered forth. He seemed very large, and like the animal of a dream, for we had given up whatever small hopes we ever had of seeing one. And now he appeared, much larger than life with his white head with black spectacles, his black collar and white saddle. (Roosevelt and Roosevelt, 1929)

For most of the time a giant panda relies on its thick coat of oily fur rather than shelter to maintain its body temperature. Captive pandas spend little time grooming themselves by licking, chewing or scratching their fur (Kleiman, 1983). Instead, they keep their coat in condition by rolling on their backs in the dirt, and will use their forepaws to rub their bellies with soil (Eisenberg and Kleiman, 1977). Captive pandas will also enter water occasionally when it is available, shaking like dogs to dry themselves when they have finished. One report (Fockelmann, 1985) claims that wild pandas regularly bathe in large ponds formed during the rainy season, and that it was at such a pond that Tangier Smith captured the animals that eventually made their way to England. Although there is no reason to suppose that wild pandas do not occasionally bathe, it is extremely unlikely that they return regularly to any particular spot for this purpose. Moreover, ponds are very rare in panda habitat since the hills are so steep that in most areas the streams run straight down the mountains and into the main rivers in a frenzied torrent. The most likely source of this particular hunter's tale is in the imagination of Tangier Smith himself, who probably felt it would confuse anyone else trying to trap pandas.

Where an animal has rested it leaves behind a pile of droppings, and counting these droppings gives a rough idea of how long an animal spends in any one site. During a typical rest of two hours, an animal may pass 20 to 25 droppings, and such bed-sites are found frequently in panda habitat. However, pandas will return several times to favourite bed-sites, and this, combined with the difficulty of tracking animals when there is no snow, makes it difficult to draw accurate conclusions about daily activity cycles by simply following trails and counting droppings.

Much more detailed data on how long a giant panda spends resting have been obtained by trapping animals and fitting them with a radio collar which is sensitive to movement. When the animal is resting, the collar transmits 75 pulses a minute. Movement trips a mercury switch in the collar, and the pulse rate changes to 100 a minute, so by listening to the transmissions field workers have been able to build up an accurate picture of just how a panda divides up its day. This shows that most rest periods are roughly two to four hours, which is what would be expected from the numbers of droppings found at rest sites, but a few are longer than six hours, especially in summer. A panda may choose to rest at any time of the day or night, though in summer there was a tendency for animals to sleep from before dawn well into the morning (Schaller *et al.*, 1985). This is in sharp contrast to the behaviour of captive animals, which spend the bulk of their time resting and only a few hours feeding. Captive animals are generally supplied with much more nutritious food than wild animals, the staple diet of bamboo being supplemented with a gruel of rice or potatoes, vegetables and ground meat, with supplementary vitamins. Under these conditions the animals at Ueno Zoo in Tokyo are generally active morning and evening, and tend to rest at night and during the middle of the day (Nakazato et al., 1985).

Identical techniques have been used to study the activity cycles of red pandas in Wolong (Johnson et al., 1988). From these studies it emerges that the red panda has a much more marked daily rhythm, being active mainly at dusk and from about 3.00 a.m. until well after dawn. This activity pattern is maintained in captivity to some extent, with animals in Zurich and Amsterdam Zoos being active early in the morning and at dusk, at least during winter (Keller, 1980). In the wild much of the day is spent resting, sometimes curled in the fork of a tree but perhaps more often inside hollow trees or stumps or at the base of a large tree. In total, red pandas may rest for more than 15 hours a day. Being largely nocturnal, secretive and relatively small, they are even more difficult to study by direct observation than the giant panda (Johnson et al., 1988). I was unusually lucky in spotting red pandas on two separate occasions during our stay in Wolong, and both animals were resting in isolated trees on a hillside which had been heavily logged. Few firs remained, and the ground was covered with a dense tangle of low-growing but almost impenetrable brambles and arrow bamboo. Almost the instant the animals climbed down from their trees they were lost from view.

The radio-collared animals have also been useful in working out the home-range size of individual animals. Each collared animal has its radio transmitter set to a different frequency, and by taking accurate bearings of each radio signal from at least three carefully mapped points, the location of every collared animal can be calculated. At least, that is the theory. In practice, the terrain is so steep and convoluted that the signal often appears to be coming from three different directions at once, and even with considerable practice it is not always possible to distinguish the true signal from echoes reflected off distant hillsides. Often the signal of only one or two animals can be heard from any one location, and so radio tracking involves hours of stiff climbing every day, up steep, muddy, sometimes downright dangerous trails, carrying a radio receiver, headphones, aerial, compass, notebook and camera (just in case). As if this were not enough, it is often raining or snowing, and almost always cold. Under these conditions, beginning in the winter of 1980, George Schaller and his group at Wolong trapped and collared six animals, and between the date of capture and August 1982 successfully located pandas on 1,561 occasions, and took a total of 28,450 activity readings. Peter Matthiessen, in his book *The Snow Leopard* quotes a letter from the curator of mammals at the American Museum of Natural History in New York City, warning of the dangers of working with Schaller.

> I look forward to learning what you and George see, hear and accomplish in a
> march through Nepal. I should warn you, the last friend I had who went walking

with George in Asia came back—or more properly, *turned* back—when his boots were full of blood . . . (Matthiessen, 1978)

After talking to biologists that have worked with him recently, it seems to me that 15 years later this is still a warning to be heeded!

This mass of data accumulated by the panda research project in Wolong shows that each giant panda has a range of between 3.9 and 6.2 km², and that the ranges of individual animals—both males and females—may overlap extensively. However, animals tend to concentrate their activity within 'core areas' of 0.3 to 0.4 km², behaviour especially true of females. This considerably reduces the possibility of animals meeting by chance, although males, with their overlapping ranges and without the females' fidelity to a well-defined core area, may be well aware of the sex, age-class and identity of other pandas in their home range. With the exception of an ageing, medium-sized male called Wei, the average distance between daily radio locations was always less than 500 m, though tracking in snow shows that animals may actually travel twice as far as this as they meander across a hillside since like most animals they do not travel in straight lines. Adult males also moved more in late winter and early spring than at other times.

Giant pandas do not maintain an exclusive territory. Once again it is safe to assume that the animals are trying to save energy, and that the costs of scent marking, calling or fighting outweigh the benefits likely to obtain from keeping other animals out. Females may be more possessive about their core area, which is usually notable for its gentle slopes and thick cover of arrow bamboo. Subadults must make do with steeper slopes and less potential food, implying competition between animals for the best range, but if there is such competition it is not clear how an animal keeps others away.

Similar observations show that female red pandas in Wolong have a home range of between 0.9 and 1.1 km², much smaller than that of the giant panda (D. G. Reid, pers. comm.). Like the giant panda, the female red panda spends much of her time in a 'core area' of some 0.26 km². Despite the broad similarity in behaviour and diet, it is unlikely that red and giant pandas in Wolong compete seriously for food. Red pandas feed almost exclusively on the leaves of arrow bamboo, while leaves are a major food source for giant pandas only between July and October. In the Langtang National Park in Nepal, home ranges of female red pandas vary between 1.0 and 1.5 km², broadly similar to that of the animals in Wolong. Males however have much larger home ranges, varying between 1.7 and 9.6 km². In Nepal, the ranges of individual animals do not overlap, except in early winter, when males travel further afield, probably in search of breeding opportunities (Yonzon and Hunter, 1989).

The lack of competition between the two species is a mark of how totally and uniquely both red and giant pandas are adapted to their habitat. It has long been fashionable to regard the giant panda as an animal ill-suited to its environment, and incompetent in almost every function crucial to its survival. How this idea gained such widespread acceptance more than a century after Darwin published *The Origin of Species* will no doubt make a fascinating study for some future historian. The reality is that although the panda may appear at first sight to be no more than a carnivore forced by circumstance to change to a bamboo diet, it is no such animal. Its teeth, for example, are typical of a herbivore, the cheek teeth large and flat with an elaborate crown pattern which enables it to bite and crush bamboo stems with speed and ease. The bones of the skull are dense and compact, the lower jaw weighing twice as much as that of a larger bear. The bone is particularly enlarged and thickened where the jaw muscles are anchored to the skull, giving the animal an immensely powerful bite. The short digestive tract, apparently so ill-equipped to handle a vegetarian diet, allows the bulky, indigestible fibre to pass through the gut in less than eight hours (Davis, 1964). In this way the giant panda can process a vast quantity of food, rather more than 10 per cent of its body weight every day (or more than a quarter of its body weight if it is feeding on shoots). True, it is inefficient at digesting bamboo stems when compared with other herbivores feeding on other plant materials, but this misses the point. In these secluded forests so diverse in animal life, it is the only animal able to make substantial use of this umpromising source of food. Even ruminant herbivores like the takin, which according to Ken Johnson of the World Wildlife Fund team will eat 'anything that gets in the way', generally avoid stems.

Another key adaptation which allows the panda to feed so efficiently on bamboo is the pseudothumb, a sixth digit which is actually not a thumb at all but rather a wristbone, the radial sesamoid. The panda's extra thumb lies beneath a pad on the animal's forepaw. Muscles normally linked to the true thumb are attached to this bone, enabling the panda to grip and manipulate bamboo in the neat, effortless way that impresses everyone fortunate enough to watch a panda feed. The evolution of the panda's thumb probably required only minor reorganisation of the bones and muscles of the hand. It may not be a great evolutionary leap, but it works.

The red panda also has a modified wristbone which acts as an extra thumb, though the red panda's thumb is poorly developed when compared with its more famous namesake. It too is well adapted to its niche. It has big molars and premolars, both wider than they are long, ideally suited to grinding down the large quantities of fibrous material it must process. This much it has in common with the giant panda, and yet, because red panda are much smaller, weighing about 6 kg, they take a rather different approach to many of the other problems associated with feeding on bamboo.

The giant panda relies on its thick coat of oily fur and its large size to conserve heat and so save energy. (A large animal has a relatively small surface area from which to radiate heat.) The red panda has an equally luxuriant coat, but its smaller body size means that it requires more food per kilogram of body weight than the giant panda, a difference it must make up in part by selecting better-quality food. The red panda also has other tricks for saving energy. It sleeps for longer than the giant panda, and casual observation suggests that whenever possible it sleeps in the sun. Also, the red panda is able to restrict the flow of blood through its skin and so lower its skin temperature. When the air temperature is near freezing, the skin temperature of

Figure 12. The giant panda's peculiar thumb. Top left is the fore-paw, showing the pseudo-thumb used to grasp bamboo stems. Below is the skeleton of the fore-paw. The pseudothumb is in fact a modified wristbone, the radial sesamoid. Top right is the hind paw for comparison.

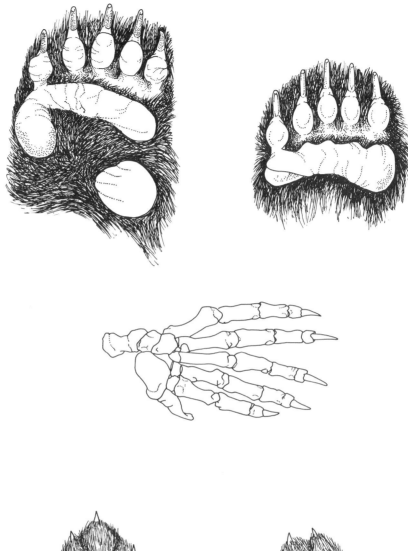

Figure 13. Paws of the red panda.

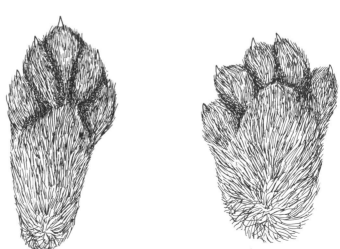

a resting red panda may be between 20 and 26°C, and may even fall as low as 15°C, which cuts down considerably the amount of heat it loses to the environment. Only when the air temperature falls below freezing does the red panda increase its metabolic rate substantially to compensate (McNab, 1988). Even so, low skin temperatures cannot be maintained for very long, probably because permanent tissue damage would result, which may explain the pattern of frequent short rests revealed by the studies of radio-collared animals.

It is the physical similarities between the red and giant pandas that have continued to fuel the long-running debate over their relationship to each other. No-one denies that there are similarities between the animals, but the question is whether these are the result of evolution from a common, recent ancestor. There are many examples in nature of animals that have independently developed similar evolutionary solutions to the same problems, a phenomenon known to biologists as convergence. One example is the similar social structures of ants and termites. These insect families are only distantly related, but in both, sterile workers tend a queen who lays all the eggs, and both produce specialised soldier castes of individuals that are prepared to die in defence of the colony. So is the similarity between the two pandas the result of a close relationship or convergence?

When Alphonse Milne-Edwards examined the specimens sent to him by Père David, he confidently rejected the idea that the panda was a bear, and grouped it instead with the red panda in the Procyonidae, the family which also contains the racoons, coatis and ringtails. Although Père David accepted the change with typical humility, other scientists were quick to disagree. In the same year Gervais (1875) published a paper placing the giant panda in the Ursidae—the bear family—with the scientific name of *Pandarctos*. For almost a hundred years eminent scientists then took it in turn to shift the beast from one family into the other and back again, with a fair number of fence-sitters who favoured erecting a separate family for both animals, with all the uncomfortable compromises that such a position entails. The score to date seems to be 19 for the bears and 18 for the racoons (Mayr, 1986)—with European authors following Gervais in making the giant panda a bear, while most English-speaking authorities accepting the subsequent revision by Mivart (1885), whose work was done in England. It is remarkable that the debate still rumbles on. Proponents of the 'bear school' might reasonably have thought the matter settled with the publication in 1964 of a massive and outstanding work by the American anatomist Dwight Davis. His monograph on the anatomy of the giant panda, based on a post-mortem study of Su Lin, gave a detailed analysis of a large number of anatomical characteristics, and showed that in each case the giant panda is a bear adapted to feed on bamboo. When Chi Chi died in London Zoo in 1972, another detailed post-mortem was carried out in which studies of the giant panda's brain anatomy, nervous system and neurochemistry all supported a relationship with the bears. And yet in the 1981 revision of their book on the giant panda, Ramona and Desmond Morris still felt that the matter was sufficiently undecided to write that 'we cannot avoid a feeling that somehow the giant panda is a counterfeit bear rather than a true one.'

Even in 1981 the evidence to support a close relationship between the red and giant pandas was thin. The Morrises point out the similarities between the teeth and skulls of the red and giant pandas, the similarities first noticed by Milne-Edwards. They add the similarity between the genitalia of the two animals—both have a short S-shaped penis pointing backwards—and draw attention to the unbearlike bleat of the giant panda and the unusual scent-gland and marking behaviour. With a complex and tenuous argument, George Schaller suggests that the reproductive strategies of the red and giant pandas are similar and retained from a small, common ancestor. Finally, there is the remarkable similarity between the structure of the fore-paws, both animals having an enlarged wristbone which they use to grasp bamboo.

This last feature, the panda's peculiar thumb, seems to be at the heart of the debate. Many students of animal behaviour who have watched red and giant pandas feeding seem so overwhelmed by the similarities in the way that the animals handle bamboo that they consider this to be unequivocal evidence in favour of a close relationship. This view has been challenged (Mayr, 1986) on the grounds that feeding behaviours are among the most flexible of all an animal's characteristics, but enough doubt might have remained to keep the argument running were it not for the evidence of molecular biology. To make sense of this evidence, one must first understand a bit of basic biochemistry.

The physical structure of all animals and plants is determined by their genes. Genes are stretches of DNA, stuck together in long strands which are tightly coiled to form the chromosomes. Using the DNA as a blueprint, cells produce the proteins which in turn decide everything from an animal's eye-colour to the length of its bones. Random changes in the structure of DNA—mutations—are the raw material of evolution. Changes at a single point along the strand can alter the protein encoded by that stretch of DNA. The change may be lethal, but every once in a while the new protein performs its function slightly better than the original, giving the animal an advantage in the struggle to survive.

How does this help determine the genealogy of the pandas? The essential point is that mutations occur at random and accumulate over time. When animals cease to interbreed and become separate species, a 'molecular clock' begins ticking, steadily notching up random mutations over time as the animals diverge from a common ancestor. The longer the clock ticks, the more differences there will be. The logic is not totally beyond criticism, since it assumes that mutations occur at the same rate in different animals, but it provides biologists with a powerful tool. The only problem is how to measure the changes.

Early attempts to measure genetic similarities were indirect and relatively crude. The first experiments of this type to be done on pandas were carried out in 1956 at Kansas University by Charles Leone and Alvin Wiens. By taking serum from the giant panda and injecting it into rabbits, they stimulated the rabbits to produce antibodies to the giant panda's blood proteins. When these antibodies were mixed with giant panda serum, they latched onto the giant panda's blood proteins to produce a classic antibody-antigen reaction. This of course was no surprise, since the blood proteins in the giant panda serum matched the rabbit antibodies precisely. But how would the antibodies to the giant panda serum react with blood proteins from related animals? Thanks to the 'molecular clock', the sera from closely related animals should contain similar blood proteins, but distantly related animals might have blood proteins so different as to be unrecognisable to the rabbit antibodies. Mixing the giant panda antiserum with serum from polar bears produced a weaker reaction, but the reaction obtained by mixing it with serum from racoons was weaker still. Repeating the experiment with antisera to polar-bear serum and to racoon serum produced the same result. According to this test, the giant panda was more closely related to bears than to racoons (Leone and Wiens, 1956).

In 1973 rather more sophisticated immunological experiments were performed with sera from four species of bear, the giant and red pandas and the racoon. This time, specific blood proteins were purified and used to stimulate the production of antibodies. Again, the experiments suggested a close relationship between the giant panda and the bears, but the position of the red panda was confused. Antibody reactions to one of the blood proteins, albumin, favoured an ancient link between the red panda and the bears. Antibody reactions to another blood protein, transferrin, put the red panda squarely in the middle between the bears and racoons. Something was clearly not quite right, and the whole debate opened up once again (Sarich, 1973).

More recently, the colossal power of modern bio-technology has been brought to bear on the subject by Stephen O'Brien's group at the National Cancer Institute in Maryland (O'Brien *et al.*, 1985). Using the technique of gel electrophoresis which employs an electric field to separate proteins that differ either in size or in the electrical charge they carry, the researchers compared 43 proteins from pandas, brown bears, spectacled bears, Asiatic black bears and racoons. Their results showed that the giant panda shared an ancestor with all the modern bears, but long after the bears had split from the racoons. The red panda however shared an ancestor with the racoons, but split from the racoon line only shortly after the bears and racoons separated.

To test their results for consistency the group used a sophisticated technique which directly compares the DNA from each animal, rather than comparing proteins. DNA–DNA hybridisation, as this technique is known, is even more sensitive. Changes in the structure of DNA do not necessarily cause changes in proteins, for two reasons. The same protein can be specified by different DNA codes, and so mutations do not always cause a change in protein structure. And not all the DNA in a cell necessarily codes for proteins. So by looking directly at the structure of DNA the researchers could effectively take into account changes in the DNA that were not evident from the protein studies. Once again, the results were the same. The giant panda is a bear, the red panda is a racoon.

In an attempt to finally end the argument, O'Brien's group also looked at the chromosomes of bears, pandas and racoons. The giant panda has only 42 chromosomes, compared with 74 in the American black bear, Asiatic

Figure 14. The ancestry of the pandas and their relatives, as determined by DNA hybridisation studies. Numbers indicate millions of years before the present.

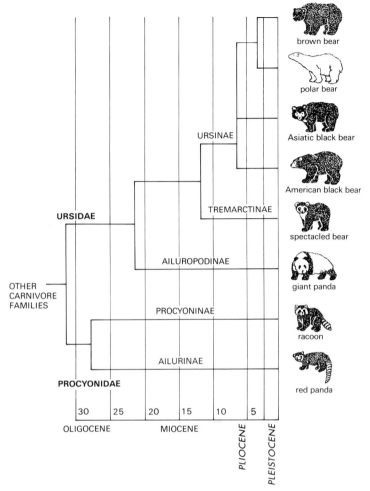

black bear and brown bear. The red panda has only 36 chromosomes, which on a simple number-count obviously places it close to the giant panda. But when the chromosomes of the giant panda and the brown bear are examined more carefully, it becomes clear that the chromosomes of the giant panda are actually bear chromosomes fused together. Once again, the giant panda is a bear.

As well as determining the structure of the family tree for bears and racoons, techniques that rely on the 'molecular clock' can be used to estimate how long ago in the earth's history one group split from another. To do this, the clock must first be calibrated by studying the rate of mutation in a group where the fossil history is well known. To calibrate the clock, the researchers used the same techniques of molecular biology to study primates, where the fossil record is well known and shows, for example, that the baboons split from the great apes some 36 million years ago, and that the gibbons split from the rest of the apes between 20 million and 25 million years ago. By comparing the DNA and proteins in the apes, the researchers could work out the rate of mutation in this group, and then assuming the rate to be the same in carnivores, could calculate the time at which branching occurred in the carnivore family tree.

The molecular studies killed the controversy for almost a month, but the case was opened again when a paper was published by another group of researchers comparing the haemoglobins of the two pandas with haemoglobin from bears and racoons. Once again, doubts were raised, since haemoglobin from the giant panda turns out to be very similar to haemoglobin from the red panda, but haemoglobin obtained from bears and racoons is quite different. In the face of the overwhelming evidence presented in O'Brien's study, most zoologists (with a few very important exceptions) are now happy to accept that this is another case of convergence. Haemoglobin is a protein from red blood cells responsible for carrying oxygen around the body, an essential function that is very sensitive to change in the protein structure. Most likely, the similarities between the haemoglobins of red and giant pandas are the result of adaptation to life at high altitude or to some other feature peculiar to the pandas' unusual lifestyle.

In what may be a forlorn attempt to settle the matter, O'Brien's group recently published a further analysis of 289 proteins. Once again, the results generally agree with their earlier studies (Goldman *et al.*, 1989). With the history of the debate so far, this is unlikely to be the final word on the subject.

11. Lighter and more agile than the giant pandas, red pandas climb easily. *(Chris Catton)*

12. Workers in Tangjiahe reserve examine a tranquillised panda. *(WWF/K. Schaller)*

13. Tracking of radio-collared animals has provided a wealth of information about their daily activity cycles, range and movements. *(WWF/ Bautert/BCL)*

4. Social Behaviour

Giant pandas are by nature solitary animals, for most of the time avoiding direct contact with others of their own kind. But at crucial stages in their lives pandas, like all solitary mammals, are forced to spend time with others. In spring males and females must seek each other out in order to mate. And in autumn the females give birth to a single cub which will be their constant companion for the next 18 months or more.

At birth a giant panda cub weighs between 90 and 130 g, about the size of a small rat. The mother will be as much as 900 times the weight of her off-spring, making giant panda cubs proportionately the smallest young of all placental mammals. Blind and naked except for a sparse covering of white fur, the new-born cub is entirely helpless. Its voice is its only protection, and almost immediately it is born the cub wails, producing a sound out of all proportion with its size. Like the crying of a human child, the noise is piercing, and in captivity it is usually this sound that first draws the mother's attention to her cub, stimulating her to pick it up and begin to nurse it.

The mother is extremely attentive, and for the first three weeks she rarely leaves the new-born unattended in the nest. When she moves away from her nest area to urinate or defecate, she carries the cub in her mouth. By two weeks the pattern of black markings is beginning to show through, first on the ears, around the eyes and on the shoulders, later on the legs, chest and neck. According to Beijing Zoo (Peking Zoo, 1974), two-week-old cubs suckle 6–12 times a day. In Wolong I watched Li Li and her cub Lam Tian for several days at this age, and found it impossible to tell whether the cub was actually at the breast or not, since it was hidden for most of the time beneath its mother's huge paw. At two weeks old, Lam Tian had stopped looking like a bald rat, and now looked more like a piglet, its pink skin still showing through the thickening coat. Its tail was surprisingly long—about a quarter the length of its body—and as Li Li licked her cub, her tongue wrapped around it. The mother's frequent licking stimulates the cub to excrete, and keeps it clean. Li Li was an obsessive mother, and would continue to lick the cub for anything between 10 and 20 minutes after a feed. Feeding and grooming over, she would pull one rear leg out from beneath herself and flop down on her side as if exhausted, still clutching the cub in her paw.

By one month old, cubs are already beginning to look like miniature adults, except for the tail which is still disproportionately long. However, the eyes remain closed most of the time, and it is not until the cub is over two months old that it begins to crawl, and not until 5–6 months does it begin to eat bamboo.

Giant pandas often give birth to twins, but in captivity at least the second cub is always ignored. In the wild it may be that a female occasionally succeeds in raising two cubs, although apart from one discovery of two small cubs in a den in the Liang mountains, the only evidence for this is an occasional sighting of a mother with two young (Schaller *et al.*, 1985). It is at least possible that in cases where a panda is seen with two youngsters they are not both her own. The China/World Wildlife Fund study suspected that one of their radio-collared animals adopted a stray cub following the death of her own young. The evidence for this is rather circumstantial, and there is no hard evidence at all that pandas adopt additional strays when their own cubs are still alive (Schaller *et al.*, 1985). Some doubt must remain about whether or not a panda in the wild can raise both of a pair of twins to maturity.

There is little information on the interactions between mother and young in the wild. Pandas give birth in a den, usually a hollow tree or a cave. Sites chosen as maternity dens must obviously be large enough for a panda to sit upright inside, and must also be surrounded by bamboo. For the first few months the cub is immobile and remains in the den, and where possible a mother chooses a den where she does not have to leave the cub unattended for long periods while she wanders in search of food. Suitable sites are consequently rare, especially in forests where the older trees have been felled for timber. One female at Wolong made her den beneath the roots of a fallen tree. Much of her range had been clear-felled and there was probably no other suitable site.

The mother sometimes drags bits of wood, saplings and branches into the den, behaviour that has also been observed in captive females about to give birth, but what purpose this serves one can only guess. Scientists studying pandas are faced with a difficult dilemma here. A maternity den provides the only opportunity for them to watch a female for an extended period, since she must continually return to her cub. A long vigil would provide a lot of fascinating data about a crucial stage in the animal's life. On the other hand there is always the possibility that an intrusion might drive the mother to abandon her cub. The result has always been a decision not to disturb the

Figure 15. Large, hollow fir trees surrounded by bamboo are the sort of den sites favoured by giant pandas. Often the female will drag a few branches into the den before giving birth, but why she does this is a mystery.

mother. The data that could be gained by watching a mother and her young would help little in securing the future of the species, and the panda's present situation is so precarious that the risk could not be justified. However, a female that gave birth near a logging camp on the edge of Fengtongzhai Reserve seemed unconcerned about people nearby, and stayed with her young even though she saw people every day.

A little information has been gleaned by studying radio-collared females that have given birth. In early September 1981, for example, one of the radio-collared animals in the Wolong Reserve gave birth. For three weeks the radio signals showed that she remained close to a large hollow tree, and on 1 September she moved into the den. Presumably, she gave birth shortly after this, and for the rest of the month the radio signals showed that she was less active than usual and remained close to the den all the time.

After a time the female leaves the den, carrying the still helpless cub in her mouth. How long she remains in the den varies considerably. Most females probably leave after one or two months, but in the Qinling mountains a 5-kg cub, which judging by the growth of captive animals would be about five months old, was found in a maternity den in April. Young are dependent on their mother at least until they are weaned at 8–9 months, and normally stay with her until they are 18 months old, behaviour that was known to native hunters as long ago as 1937 but has only recently been confirmed by Western zoologists (Carter, 1937). Next to nothing is known about their behaviour during this period, but the cub must be carried around until it is old enough to walk on its own, a stage reached by captives at about four months. In April 1987 I came across a mother and her cub in the Wolong Reserve. The cub was sitting in a birch tree, and did not see me as I approached. I sat and watched it for about an hour, much of which it spent playing with a stick. Sitting in a fork that looked barely capable of taking the weight, the cub rolled on its back and bit at the stick, juggling it in its forepaws. Eventually and inevitably the stick fell from its grasp, at which the cub sat upright and peered into the bamboo below looking for all the world like a child that has just dropped its favourite toy over the side of its pram. Below I could hear the mother chewing contentedly on stems of umbrella bamboo. In all this time neither mother nor cub made any other sound, until a shift in the wind carried my scent in their direction. The mother moved off 10 to 15 m in the other direction, turned towards me and snorted, and then disappeared into the bamboo leaving her cub in the tree. The cub remained where it was until I moved out of sight. When I looked back a few minutes later, it too had gone.

The first months of life are the most dangerous for pandas, as for most animals. In its den a cub risks predation by stoats, weasels, yellow-throated martens and golden cats. Once it emerges into the outside world it faces new risks. Martens and brown bears could easily catch and kill young cubs. Dholes—Asian wild dogs which usually hunt in packs of between 5 and 12 animals—would have little trouble in bringing down an infant, and there is even a record of them killing and eating an old panda in the Tangjiahe Reserve.

By its second winter a young panda is already quite large enough to defend itself against most of its potential predators, its sharp claws and large canines equipping it to see off all but the most determined of attackers. Although rarely aggressive, several captive pandas have shown themselves proficient in the use of these weapons when the mood takes them. In 1964 the normally docile Chi Chi surprised everyone at London Zoo by attacking and wounding one of her young keepers. In Chicago Zoo Mei Lan inflicted such serious injuries on a keeper that his arm had to be amputated, and more recently Washington Zoo's Ling Ling attacked and wounded one of her keepers. Giant pandas can move with remarkable speed when aroused, but they usually appear to show little concern when threatened. Their nonchalant behaviour in the face of danger obviously astonished William Sheldon:

> On one occasion at a distance of 350 yards I observed two individuals on the edge of a bamboo jungle. Driven out by four dogs and warned by several high-powered bullets whistling about them, neither animal even broke into a run. The gait was a determined and leisurely walk. Again, Dean Sage and I observed another panda pursued by four dogs. In this instance he *walked* to within eight feet of Dean and was stopped only by bullets. He gave absolutely no evidence that he saw either of us, and seemed completely to disregard both the shots and the loud talking and shouts of a few minutes previous. During the course of tracking different animals for several miles I never saw a sign of one travelling faster than a walk. (Sheldon, 1937)

Sheldon interpreted this as evidence that the giant panda is 'an extremely stupid beast' but it would be truer to say that it has little to fear and so has no need to waste energy in hurrying itself. In their present range, adults and subadults are at risk only from leopards, and of course man. One of the first pandas ever held in captivity at Beijing Zoo carried the scars of a fight with a leopard (T'an, 1958), and the study in the Wolong Reserve found three leopard droppings which contained panda hair and bone. The remains in two of the droppings were infants, but the third was of a two-year-old animal. Pandas are only a minor component of the leopard's diet, their main prey being tufted deer.

It was long thought that the giant panda's black and white coat might act as camouflage, but this theory has several flaws. First, the coat provides camouflage only in winter, when the ground is covered in snow, and for the rest of the year it makes the animal very conspicuous. The markings make the cub stand out against the blackness in its maternity den whatever the weather outside, and when it emerges into the world the coat provides little protection. A cub's response to danger is to climb a tree, even when there is snow lying on the ground. Any snow on the branches that might have helped it blend inconspicuously into the background will be knocked off during the process, for panda cubs are not stealthy climbers. The giant panda's black and white coat makes it conspicuous to predators when it is most vulnerable, and much of the panda's historic range received far less snow than its present refuge. Even in its present range, other animals at far greater risk from predators—musk deer and serow, for example—are more conventionally coloured and far more difficult to spot for most of the year.

If the coat is not an effective camouflage, then what could its role possibly be? One idea has been that it has something to do with temperature control. A black surface both absorbs and radiates more heat than a white one. When the sun is shining animals can sunbathe and black animals will warm up more quickly; on the other hand it is more difficult for black animals to maintain their body temperature on cold, dull days (Hamilton and Heppner, 1967; Stullken and Hiestand, 1953). If pandas were black on top and white beneath, the theory would be more credible, but it hardly explains the detailed pattern of the giant panda's coat. Before zoologists became fully aware of the importance of social interactions in the lives of animals, similar functional explanations were used in an attempt to explain the equally distinctive coat of the zebra.

It is hard to imagine an animal more conspicuous than a zebra on the plains of Africa. Even artists have trouble trying to make a convincing case for their stripes as camouflage amongst long grass, and the zebra's behaviour is calculated to make them as obvious as possible both to predators and to each other. They never attempt to conceal themselves, and prefer to graze in large herds, exposed in an area where they have an excellent view of their surroundings. Their response to the sight of a lion or leopard is not to freeze in an attempt to blend with their surroundings, but to gather together into a group and move slowly away from the threat, outrunning their hunters only should the need arise.

The stripes of zebras most likely evolved not for camouflage, but for social reasons. They make all members of a herd conspicuous to each other and so help to keep the group together. The distinctive black and white patterning of the giant panda cannot serve exactly the same function, since for most of their lives pandas are solitary animals. But it seems likely that the black and white markings serve a signalling function, sending a warning to other species, or social signals to their own kind. Alternative explanations make little sense.

Giant pandas generally avoid contact with each other in the wild. In their dense habitat their coat may help make animals conspicuous to each other and prevent them from surprising themselves by approaching too close to another of their own kind. It is usually assumed that the giant panda's eyesight is poor, but there is actually little solid evidence for this. Like bears, they often appear not to see humans, but in the case of bears it is now accepted that this is not the result of poor vision but deliberate 'ignoring behaviour'. To stare directly at an intruder is a threat, and bears foraging close to each other deliberately avoid looking in the direction of other animals nearby. It is quite possible that the same is true for pandas. The pupil of the giant panda's eye is a cat-like vertical slit, a more efficient means of regulating the light reaching the retina. This suggests that the retina is very sensitive to light, which would account for the animal's apparently excellent night vision. There is no good reason to assume that their day-time vision is consequently poor.

Except for the behaviour of mating groups, almost all the information on social behaviour comes from the observation of captives introduced to each other under extremely artificial conditions. None the less, these encounters have proved useful to the extent that they tell us a good deal about the

Figure 16. Aggressive and submissive postures in red pandas. Red pandas signal submission with head held low and ears flattened. Aggression is signalled with head high and ears pricked.

Figure 17. A giant panda threatening an intruder adopts a posture quite different from that of the red panda. Seen head on, the ears are outlined against the white of the neck, reinforcing the effect of the black eye-patches.

things pandas do not do. Facial expressions seem to play little part in social interactions, for example. Unlike most carnivores, giant pandas do not move their ears to signify fear or aggression, nor do they erect their hair as a threat. Instead, aggression is signalled by lowering the head and staring at the opponent, a posture which as George Schaller points out duplicates the distinct eye-patches by outlining the black ears against the white neck (Schaller *et al.*, 1985). To signal submissiveness, a panda will put its head between its front legs, often hiding its eye-patches with its paw. This position is adopted by females during mating, and also by captive animals that are being harrassed by humans—particularly vets with anaesthetic darts. At close range aggression is signalled by a swipe with a paw, or by a low-pitched growl or bark that will send an opponent scampering up the nearest tree.

Red pandas signal their social intent quite differently. Studies of captives at Zurich Zoo show that red pandas signal aggression by lifting their heads and cocking their ears, while the posture with head held low and ears flattened back signals submission. The face of the red panda is much more mobile, and the varied facial markings may allow different animals to recognise each other visually. Animals that are acquainted will either ignore each other or move closer to sniff at each other. Strangers on the other hand will hiss and stand upright to threaten each other. This may escalate into a full-blown fight, the animals hitting out with their fore-paws and attempting to bite each other on the back or rump. When one animal retreats, the contest is over (Keller, 1980).

It is not obvious from the studies that have been done with captives whether or not giant pandas can recognise each other as individuals on sight, largely because there have been so few meetings between total strangers in zoos outside China. However, there is indirect evidence which suggests that in the wild, giant pandas recognise other animals as individuals and act accordingly. On the morning of 27 March 1987 two Chinese workers set off as usual from the research camp in Wolong to locate the radio-collared animals. After walking for an hour, they heard pandas fighting not far from the trail. Very fortunately both pandas were radio collared, one an adult male, Hua Hua, the other an adult female, Xin Yue, who was known to have a six-month-old cub.

Pandas do not normally come into season while raising a cub born in the previous autumn, so although males fight for access to oestrus females at this time of year, this could hardly explain the commotion. Running towards the source of the sound, the workers soon found part of the answer. In the snow lay a dead panda cub, surrounded by tufts of panda hair. A jumble of panda tracks and trampled bamboo pointed to a fierce struggle between the two adults. The intestines of the cub had been ripped out, and its hind leg bitten clean through below the knee. Claws on both front paws were ripped and bleeding, one torn off completely at the knuckle, suggesting that the cub too had put up a fight before it died.

At first it was thought that the cub might have been attacked and killed by a golden cat or leopard and the body found and partly eaten by the male panda. But although golden cat tracks had been found in the snow on the previous night, there were no signs of tracks around the body apart from those of the two pandas. It is doubtful if a golden cat could kill a six-month-old cub anyway, and a post-mortem revealed a hole through the cub's skull that had apparently been inflicted by a canine tooth. The most likely explanation is that the cub had been found and killed by the male giant panda, Hua Hua (Catton, 1987).

Infanticide by males is now well documented in several groups of animals. Male Langur monkeys attempt to kill the young of the previous male when they take over a new troop (Hrdy, 1974). Lions do the same when they take over a new pride (Schaller, 1963). Infanticide has also been reported in bears. In brown bears, for example, between 10 and 40 per cent of all cubs will die during the first 18 months of life, often as a result of attacks from adult males (Domico, 1988). In each case the evolutionary advantage to the infanticidal male is clear. By killing the young, he removes animals that will compete with his own offspring. More importantly, he brings the female into oestrus. While the mother is lactating, ovulation is inhibited, and does not begin again until the demand for milk ceases. (This delay in the resumption of cycling is a well-known phenomenon in humans, and although the inhibition of ovulation is not complete and depends on the nutritional state of the mother, the trend is the same.)

Xin Yue did indeed come back into season that summer, and was observed to mate with an uncollared male on 22 May, less than two months after losing her cub. For this act of infanticide to make evolutionary sense, Hua Hua must have been able to recognise Xin Yue and remember that he had not mated with her during the previous summer, or alternatively to recognise somehow that the cub was not his kin. From an evolutionary perspective, the whole purpose of reproduction is to pass on an individual's genes to the next generation, and unless Hua Hua could be certain that he was not the father of the cub, the risk of perhaps killing his own offspring would certainly outweigh the potential benefit of bringing Xin Yue into season a year early in the hope that he might be able to mate with her.

Hua Hua's behaviour can be explained only if pandas recognise their kin, or recognise each other as individuals and remember events that took place a year previously. This would have seemed a ridiculous suggestion to the early panda hunters. Even now the evidence is admittedly weak, but there is one other anecdote which indicates that pandas have excellent memories. As mentioned previously, London Zoo's Chi Chi once attacked one of her keepers, Christopher Madden, pinning him down and viciously savaging his right leg. The keeper was rescued by a colleague, who distracted Chi Chi's attention by clouting her across the head with a broom. It was seven months before Madden's leg healed sufficiently for him to return to work, but Chi Chi recognised him immediately and began growling and pacing up and down in her enclosure as soon as he reappeared.

It is not clear whether visual cues or smell are more important in allowing giant pandas to recognise each other. In the wild and in captivity giant pandas scent-mark regularly. Both males and females have a large area of naked, glandular skin surrounding the anogenital region which exudes a thick, dark secretion. In captivity animals repeatedly mark selected spots in their enclosures. To mark a horizontal surface—a protruding stone for example—

copy
of scent
marking

the panda squa⟨...⟩ar end across the ground.
Vertical surface⟨...⟩ump—are usually marked
by cocking one ⟨...⟩gion. More rarely, an animal walks backw⟨...⟩a handstand on its front
paws. It then rub⟨...⟩⟨...⟩on the tree, leaving a scent mark
more than a met⟨...⟩above the ground. I have also watched an adult male
released into a novel enclosure scent-mark a thin larch tree while lying on
his back with his rear legs astride the trunk. Often this scent marking is
reinforced with urine, and George Schaller notes that this urine has 'a
powerful musky odor, quite unlike normal urine' (Schaller *et al.*, 1985). In
captivity animals sometimes urinate on marking-sites without rubbing on
them at all.

In Wolong many trees had been used as marking-posts at one time or
another, particularly along the crests of ridges. Fir trees are the favoured
marking-sites, and on well used posts the lower area had sometimes been
rubbed smooth and darkened by the build-up of secretions. Most posts also
showed claw marks, often no more than scratches as if the animal had
merely brushed the back with his paw. Trees marked after snow usually
revealed no more than a few scraps of moss and bark which might well have
been knocked off as the animal rubbed his hind quarters, since animals
rarely use their full marking repertoire.

As well as marking some trees repeatedly so that secretions build up on
the tree, pandas mark trees that show no sign of ever having been marked
before. These trees are often close to a path, as in the case of a prominent
magnolia marked in the height of the breeding season at Wolong which
had been so deeply raked by a giant panda's claws that resin poured from the
wound for several days afterwards. As well as this deliberate signalling, pandas mark their passage through an area by leaving droppings, and a panda
travelling through strange territory must be continually assaulted by a
battery of smells that provide detailed information on the sex and social
status of the present tenants.

In captivity males scent-mark much more frequently than females, and
marking is more frequent during spring as the reproductive season
approaches (Kleiman *et al.*, 1979). In the wild too there is a significant
increase in marking activity in winter and spring, and it is not clear whether
the animals scent-mark at all during the summer months. In Wolong it
seems that females have only a single oestrus period each year, between
mid-March and mid-May, while in the Qinling mountains there may also be
a second oestrus period between September and November (Yong, 1981).
Captive animals may also show weak signs of oestrus in the autumn. Radio-
tracking shows that during the winter and spring, males move about in their
range much more than females, presumably seeking to make contact with
females as they come into season. As the breeding season approaches, the
male's behaviour seems to become almost frantic, travelling further and
marking more often so that walking through the forest after a snowfall the
evidence of their activities gives the impression that they have suddenly
become quite common.

Throughout April 1987 I kept a detailed account of the movements of

Figure 18. Scent-marking postures in the giant panda.

two radio-collared animals, the male Hua Hua, and a female named Xin Xing. We had hoped to locate and film a mating group in the wild, an event which has been observed several times by the scientists at Wolong. For the few days in which a female shows signs of oestrus, the pandas cease to be elusive and pay little attention to humans. Instead, they become totally engrossed in their own kind, which we hoped would give us a chance to obtain a unique film record. With this as the only object, my methods were more arbitrary than those of the scientists, but they consequently provided some interesting results.

On 1 April Xin Xing was somewhere on a precipitous ridge above the main river valley. About 2 km away, near the crest of another ridge, the researchers had located a second, uncollared female who had already taken up residence in a site where matings had been observed in previous years. During the next month the females stayed more or less in the same place, while Hua Hua spent much of his time travelling backwards and forwards between them. On 8 April, he was close to the uncollared female on her ridge, but by the next morning he had moved close to Xin Xing. On the morning of 10 April he was still close to Xin Xing, but during the day he moved back to the uncollared female again. He continued trotting backwards and forwards between the two, an exhausting tramp up one steep ridge down into a deep valley and up the other side. Throughout this time until his radio collar failed on 21 April he never spent more than a couple of days in the same area. Three days after his radio transmissions ceased, villagers heard the sounds of pandas fighting at night, close to Xin Xing's bamboo patch. Previous observations had shown that males often fight over oestrous females, but by the time we arrived the next day the area was quiet. Our only consolation was that even if we had indeed missed Xin Xing's mating, we could not have filmed at night anyway.

Except when courting and mating, giant pandas make little sound. Pandas often snort when approached by humans or other pandas, but apart from this and the cries of very young cubs the animals are more or less silent except during the breeding season. At this time, pandas produce a rich repertoire of sounds. The roar, bark and moan are loud sounds, all audible at more than a kilometre. Many of the giant panda's loud vocalisations have strong, low-frequency components (Zhu and Meng, 1987). Low-frequency sounds tend to carry further in dense forest than high frequencies, and these calls are probably long-distance advertising calls although their exact function is far from clear. Females about to come into oestrus often take up a position on an exposed ridge, from which sound carries into surrounding valleys. These sounds attract other males and so increase male competition for the female. A female consequently improves her chances of mating with the healthiest and strongest male, the best available father for her cub. The difficulty with this explanation is that from the reports published so far it is the males that appear to make most of the noise, and if the sole function of calling is to attract other males, they would do better to keep quiet.

Males can spend several days 'keeping company' with a female about to come into season, and by the time peak oestrus approaches there may be four or five gathered around her, all anxious to mate. Scent-marking and vocalisation probably both signal subtle changes in the female's condition to the waiting males. As oestrus approaches, the female scent-marks more often and begins to produce sounds that are not heard at other times of the year. Most noticeable and unbearlike of these is the bleat, very similar to the sound of a domestic goat. During the peak period of receptivity the female also produces a 'chirp', a short call surprisingly high pitched for an animal the size of a panda. Captive females chirp when presenting to a male and when being mounted.

The behaviour of the female during this pre-oestrus period may be important in stimulating hormonal changes in the male, bringing him into reproductive condition. When a captive male is introduced to an oestrous female, the level of male hormones in his urine rises, reaching a sudden peak when the female is at her most receptive and decreasing just as rapidly after mating is over.

Judging by the behaviour of captives, females approaching oestrus either fend off an approaching male or run away, swatting and biting any male that comes too close. As oestrus develops the female becomes less aggressive, and eventually she begins to follow the male and present to him with her tail lifted. If the male is reluctant, she will back into him—behaviour which is presumably intended to stimulate him sexually. These behavioural changes provide the only obvious indication for human observers that the female is indeed in oestrus.

Once the female reaches peak oestrus she stops pursuing the male and allows him to mount, adopting the position usually known as lordosis, with her tail raised and head lowered. The male squats or stands behind the female with his front paws on her back, and copulates for between half a minute and five minutes, sometimes mouthing at the female's neck as he does so. As he dismounts the female may turn and bite at him, although she sometimes just walks away.

According to Chinese workers at Wolong who have now observed several wild matings, most roughly follow the pattern of the encounter observed by Zhao Cannan and Wang Xueqing in April 1983.

> A female sits in a fir about 10 m above ground. Wei (an adult male) bleats near the base of the tree. He climbs 3 m up the tree but 5 minutes later descends and, in walking away, passes the observers at 2 m. Another male, large and uncollared and with blood on forehead and ear, approaches then chases Wei a short distance. Wei, however, returns and once more climbs the tree in which the female sits; he bleats, she moans. Two minutes later, Wei descends. An uncollared male is now near the tree too, as is the male Pi. The latter two face each other, moan, roar and tussle until the uncollared male withdraws . . . Pi ascends the fir and mounts the female, she crouched, bridging two branches, he balanced by her rump . . . Mean-while yet another male has appeared and the three squabble around the base of the tree. Pi and the female descend, mill around with the others, then climb back and sit 1–3 m apart. Once the female roars at Pi . . . Later he first seems to embrace her without trying to copulate, then reclines, gently pawing her back while she squats by his legs. A fifth male arrives . . . Pi descends and walks out of sight, and 3 minutes later the female does so too. (Schaller *et al.*, 1985)

The next day there were still several pandas around the female, and although Pi was the dominant male, two of the subordinates succeeded in mating with the female. Multiple mating has several possible advantages for the female. It improves the chances that she will be fertilised, since there is always a small risk that the dominant male might be infertile. And it con-fuses the issue of paternity, which would reduce the risk of infanticide by other males in the area. All the males that succeed in mating have at least some chance of fathering a cub, and so gain nothing by killing the cub should they get the chance at a later date. But none of this explains why Pi made no attempt to prevent further matings, unless the female was able to conceive only during the brief period he spent with her. In some animals the semen of the first male to mate with a female forms a plug in the neck of the cervix which makes it difficult for the sperm of subsequent males to make their way to the egg, but giant pandas have no accessory glands in their urogenital system and do not produce a large volume of sperm. Per-haps male pandas cannot spare the energy for the prolonged battles that would be involved in preventing other males from mating, or perhaps females have more control over which males they mate with than the reports published to date suggest. At the moment we can only speculate, and await the results of further field studies.

Among captive animals at Beijing Zoo, the time between mating and birth varies from 122 to 163 days, with an average of about 140 days, although cubs have been born after as little as 96 days or as much as 168 days. This suggests that when the female has been fertilised the embryo does not begin to develop immediately, a theory that is supported by studies on captives which show that hormones usually associated with pregnancy are not detectable until 5–6 weeks before birth (Chaudhuri *et al.*, 1988).

Delayed development of the embryo is known to occur in a wide variety of animal species. It allows animals to adjust the interval between mating and birth so that courtship, mating and lactation occur at a time which suits the female. Many seals, for example, haul out onto their beaches or ice floes only once each year, and in their brief time out of the water they give birth to one pup and conceive the next. The gestation period of the pup is only 4 to 6 months, and in order to fit reproduction into an annual cycle, development of the embryo is suspended for 6 to 8 months. Eurasian badgers give birth in spring, so that the heaviest demand on the females' milk supply occurs when food is plentiful. The gestation period is only 8 weeks, and if the embryo began to develop immediately this would require the animals to mate in mid-winter when they are usually inactive. Instead, they mate at any time between February and October, and when the embryo has divided to form a hollow ball of cells it enters a state of suspended animation and floats free in the uterus for several months. When the time is right—signalled by the increasing day length as mid-winter passes—the embryo implants into the wall of the uterus, and resumes its development.

Delayed implantation has no obvious advantages for giant pandas. Females give birth during August and September when foraging mostly on nutritious bamboo leaves, but there is no obvious reason why this birth season could not be achieved by matings in June and July followed by a normal pregnancy. George Schaller argues that delayed implantation might give the species flexibility, which could have allowed the panda to adapt to a variety of conditions in its larger historical range. However, even in its present range the giant panda utilises a wide variety of bamboo species which shoot in different seasons, and yet there is little seasonal variation in mating or birth times. Alternatively, the mechanism might allow females to respond to changes in the quality of their food, so that if food quality remains low during the autumn, the embryo might fail to implant (Schaller, 1985). This would save the female the energetic drain of an undesirable pregnancy, but there is no evidence that birth-rates were reduced following the bamboo flowering in Wolong, when presumably the pandas were under nutritional stress.

Not all peculiarities of an animal's lifestyle or physiology are necessarily adaptations that improve its chances of survival. Some characteristics—the human appendix, for example—are of no benefit to their owners but are simply evidence of the animal's evolutionary past. It is not difficult to see how delayed implantation might have been of benefit to the panda's carnivorous and omnivorous ancestors. In temperate climates prey and nutritious plant food are seasonal, an abundant summer inevitably followed by winter scarcity. Black bears, brown bears and polar bears have all adapted to the annual cycle of feast and famine by laying down substantial fat reserves during the summer and remaining dormant through the winter. During this period the animals do not feed, defecate or urinate, their body temperature drops, and they live entirely on the stored reserves of fat. Over the course of the winter a black bear will lose a quarter of its body weight. For these animals it is essential that the young are born early in the year, so that the most energetically demanding period of lactation is over in time for the female to replenish her fat supply before the winter sets in. In all cases this is achieved by mating during the summer and then delaying implantation of the embryo so that the young are born early in the year. All bears living in temperate climates give birth to young which are small in relation to their mother and poorly developed, and so although they remain in the den with the female for several months, their feeding does not make great demands on her at this stage. If a female has not laid down enough fat to survive the winter and raise her cub, the embryo does not implant and no young are born.

The giant panda, surrounded throughout the year with food, has no need to remain dormant in winter. Equally importantly, its food is of such poor quality that it cannot lay down large quantities of fat at any season, nor is there any time at which the quality of its food increases dramatically. The female never has much energy to spare for pregnancy or lactation, a problem which she overcomes by giving birth to small, poorly developed young which grow extremely slowly. Bears manage to raise two or three cubs, but it is unlikely that a giant panda can raise more than a single cub at a time —probably also an adaptation to the continuous but poor-quality food supply.

In captivity red pandas mate between early January and mid-March, and what little information is available suggests that in the wild the mating season is the same, since births occur in June and July both in Nepal and in the western portion of their range (Roberts and Kessler, 1979; D. G. Reid, pers. comm.). Red pandas have glandular pores on the soles of the feet and adults of both sexes possess paired anal glands that release a pungent, oily fluid. The glands on the feet leave scent trails that can be followed by other red pandas, and the secretions from the anal glands are rubbed on prominent marking sites. In captivity, males scent-mark more often than females, although female marking behaviour increases with the onset of breeding which may indicate that female scent-marking indicates breeding condition and receptivity. In the wild, scent marks may also act as signposts, helping an animal find its way around its range, and communicating its occupancy and social status to others in the vicinity (Conover and Gittleman, 1989).

Figure 19. Red panda scent-marking.

Red pandas concentrate their sexual activity around the time of the new moon, but the length of gestation is variable and so births are not synchronised. It is unclear what red pandas gain by using this cue to synchronise mating. Mating is concentrated into a single 24-hour period in captivity, and in the wild oestrus is probably brief. Synchronising oestrus with the new moon may help these rather solitary animals to co-ordinate their reproductive activity and improve the chances of a female finding a mate. In captivity male red pandas begin sniffing and following the trails of a female in mid-January, and from mid-January to mid-March both males and females scent-mark more often than at other times of the year. Although normally silent, captive animals occasionally produce a high-pitched twitter during the period immediately before copulation, and in the wild this call may help animals to locate each other and to reduce aggression (Roberts and Kessler, 1979). The female solicits copulation by adopting the lordosis position with head down, back arched, and tail shifted to one side. The male mounts standing behind the female on his hind legs and clasping her about the abdomen. Mounts may last from 2 to 20 minutes, with several bouts of thrusting and apparently several ejaculations. During the period between bouts of thrusting the male licks and grooms the back, neck and sides of the female.

The young are born between 112 and 158 days after mating, with a mean gestation length of 134 days. This variation suggests that as with the giant panda implantation of the embryo may be delayed, although there have been no hormonal studies and so the evidence for delayed implantation is not as strong as it is in the giant panda.

In the wild, red pandas use hollow trees and small caves as nest sites, into which they carry sticks, leaves and grasses for bedding. In captivity this nest-building begins several days before the young are born, and continues after birth until the young emerge from the nest. In the northern hemisphere births can occur at any time between May and August, but almost 80 per cent of all births occur in June.

At birth red panda cubs weigh between 110 and 130 g, averaging slightly larger than the cubs of giant pandas even though at an average weight of 97 kg the female giant panda is 20 times heavier than a female red panda. The litter can be anything between one and four cubs, although two is usual. They are born with eyes closed, but unlike the cubs of the giant panda are covered in a thick, dense, grey-buff fur. For the first three weeks the female remains with the young, leaving them only to eat, drink and defecate. The young grow relatively quickly, their eyes opening after 18 days, and at a little over two months they look like miniature adults. At this stage, the mother spends much more time away from the nest, returning periodically to check her cubs, or when summoned by their high-pitched whistles of distress. By three months they can climb proficiently and are ready to leave the nest and begin to take solid food.

The growth of red panda cubs apparently places a huge burden on the digestive system of their mother. Captive animals feed more often, more quickly, and for longer when lactating, in a desperate effort to keep up with the demands of their offspring. Instead of carefully nipping off a single leaf,

14. Li Li with her ten week old cub Lam Tian, the first born at the panda breeding station in Wolong. *(WWF/ J. Mackinnon)*

15. Madrid zoo's Shao Shao with Chu Lin, the first cub to be born outside China by artificial insemination. *(Harry Moore. Institute of Zoology, London)*

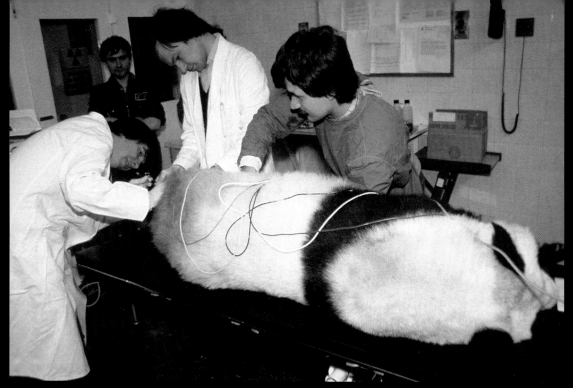

16. Despite a growing understanding of giant panda reproductive biology, captive breeding alone will not secure the future of the species. *(Harry Moore, Institute of Zoology, London)*

17. Illegal timber cutting in Langtang national park, Nepal. Deforestation has already destroyed large areas of red panda habitat in the Himalayas. *(Mark Boulton/ICCE)*

a lactating red panda takes mouthfuls of between two and five leaves at a time, a change in feeding behaviour which enables them to eat almost three times as much bamboo in the same period of foraging (Gittleman, 1988). Even so, red panda cubs grow slowly when compared with other, similar-sized animals like the racoon. Since hand-reared young grow more quickly, it is likely that this slow rate of development is a result of the mother's limited capacity to supply milk, a consequence of the problems associated with processing a herbivorous diet with a carnivore's digestive system (Gittleman, 1987).

By about 13 weeks the young are no longer dependent on their mother's milk, although they may continue to suckle occasionally until they are five months old. In captivity females do not become intolerant of the young until the approach of the breeding season in the following year, although in the wild the young probably disperse before this. In captivity the young become sexually mature at between 18 and 20 months, and females give birth to their first litter at approximately two years of age.

In captivity red pandas have survived for up to 14 years, although most animals die at 10 to 11 years. Giant pandas by contrast reach sexual maturity at about 6 or 7 years and Li Li, who became the first giant panda to give birth in captivity, in 1963, is thought to have been 30 years old when she died in 1982. Essentially, the reproductive habits of both giant and lesser pandas are similar, and typical of large animals inhabiting stable habitats in which there is keen competition for consistent but limited resources. They are relatively long-lived and slow to mature; they produce few young which are carefully nurtured; and if left undisturbed they maintain a stable population close to the maximum that the available resources can support. Unfortunately, the same reproductive parameters make their conservation one of the great challenges of the late twentieth century now that their naturally stable environment has been so dramatically disturbed by man.

5. Captive Breeding

For the public that flocked to see the collections in the first great zoos, every exhibit provided a fresh experience. Many of the animals had only recently been described by science, and each year brought new and more outlandish discoveries. When the Jardin des Plantes was founded in 1793 in Paris, to be followed by London Zoo in 1828 and Berlin Zoo in 1844, their rôle was undisputed. By housing the curiosities of the animal kingdom from around the world, the zoos would be a symbol of colonial power and a source of enlightenment for the general public. It was of no consequence that many of the animals died as a result of inadequate care. There were plenty more in the wild, and to explain modern concepts of conservation, cruelty or animal rights to the zoos' owners or to the public would have involved them in an impossible exercise in mental gymnastics. Before the abolition of slavery and child labour it would have seemed ridiculous to suggest that there might be something immoral about chaining an elephant permanently by its foot.

Zoos still depend on our fascination for exotic animals to draw the crowds through their turnstiles, but changing attitudes towards our treatment of our own species have been followed by a growing feeling that entertainment and profit are not sufficient justifications for keeping wild animals in captivity. The zoo's critics argue that by keeping rare animals on display to the public, they create a false sense that all is well with the world, and that since zoos worldwide have space and resources to protect at most 800 key species, money would be better spent on the conservation of habitat (Cohn, 1988). Zoos are now expected to perform a difficult balancing act, weighing the benefits of education, research and conservation against the harm caused to the animals themselves through their confinement.

This balance must be assessed separately for each species, and for many captivity is difficult to justify. Polar bears are not threatened in the wild, and often appear disturbed in captivity. The concrete pens needed to contain them can give the visitor little idea of their arctic habitat and the stereotyped, robotic behaviour of many captive animals is a sad corruption of their natural grace and power. Similar neurotic behaviour has been noticed in many other species, such as wolves, tigers, monkeys—the list is a long one. Desperate for stimulation, some bears in captivity have begged so much food from their admiring crowds that they have killed themselves through gross overfeeding. At the other end of the spectrum are animals like Père David's deer that have been saved from certain extinction by captive breeding.

Just where the giant panda lies in this spectrum is a matter of considerable controversy. Like polar bears, giant pandas usually range over a large area, covering distances of more than a kilometre every day, but captive-bred giant pandas and animals captured as cubs often adapt well to life in a cage, apparently enjoying the company of their keepers and happy to perform for the public. However, different animals have different temperaments, and even some animals captured young appear distressed by their confinement and exhibit repetitive, stereotyped behaviour similar to that seen in polar bears. Against the stress caused to individual animals must be weighed the benefits that their captivity might bring for the whole species. Were it not for the publicity surrounding the capture of the first zoo animals, and the 'panda-diplomacy' of recent decades, it is unlikely that the giant panda could have become the powerful symbol of conservation it is today. Pandas in captivity help to reinforce this symbolism each time they are visited by a new class of schoolchildren. Each year the press and television provide free advertising to remind a wider audience of the animals' plight with play-by-play coverage of courtship, mating, pregnancy, birth and death. No doubt some of this coverage makes many committed conservationists wince ('Pandas' f'Lings make cub fans Hsing' was one headline to announce the mating of Hsing Hsing and Ling Ling at Washington Zoo). However, it will take much more than the commitment of the already converted to slow the present rate of global destruction. That will take the backing of politicians and large quantities of cash. In the short term at least, one of the main contributions of captive pandas to the survival of their wild cousins may be their ability to earn hard currency.

The quantity of cash that a panda can generate is quite astonishing. As long ago as 1958 Chi Chi was reportedly netting $US 2,000 a week on her tour of Europe—a weekly wage which as the *New York Times* pointed out on 11 July of that year valued her at four times the worth of American Secretary of State John Foster Dulles. Not surprisingly, many deals are fairly well-kept secrets but for a 3 to 6 months' loan of a pair of pandas to foreign zoos, the Chinese now charge a fee between $US 300,000 to $US 600,000. This fee is easily recovered by most zoos. A six-month visit by Basi and Yuan Yuan to San Diego Zoo which ended in February 1988 increased attendance by 35 per cent and income by over $US 5 million. In recent years such 'rent a panda' deals have brought pandas to Los Angeles, San Francisco, Toronto, the Bronx Zoo in New York, Calgary, Dublin, the Netherlands, Fukuoka in Japan, Hong Kong and Australia. In 1988 negotiations were under way to supply animals to Atlanta, Columbus, Omaha, Portland, Seattle, Disneyworld and Michigan State Fair, and it looked as if pandas would soon be opening drive-through snack-bars and hairdressing salons, bought in by anyone wanting to attract a crowd.

When Yong Yong showed signs of oestrus during her stay at the Bronx Zoo in 1987, the World Wildlife Fund decided that the time had come to try and curtail the practice, which despite Chinese assurances to the contrary had now demonstrably led to a lost mating opportunity. At a little over a year old, Yong Yong's partner Ling Ling was far too young to mate with her. In May 1988 the World Wildlife Fund and the American Association of Zoological Parks and Aquariums began legal action to try and prevent two pandas being exhibited at the Toledo Zoo, charging that the exhibition was in breach of the Endangered Species Act. Amid accusations by both sides of crass motives and publicity-seeking, the case failed and the exhibition went ahead, but the Chinese were, not surprisingly, insulted by the implied criticism. The Toledo Zoo were none too pleased either when the success of a subsequent injunction prevented the zoo from collecting additional fees for the panda exhibit (UPI, 20 July 1988).

Attempting to tighten up the regulations, the Chinese government announced in June 1988 that in future only animals captured or artificially bred before 1983 would be allowed out of China, and that all future applications for panda loans would have to be approved by the central Chinese government. The new regulations would also insist that the zoos concerned provided funds or technical assistance to the Chinese Association for Zoological Gardens. The United States Fish and Wildlife Service apparently also changed its own policy, and a month later they refused an application by the Michigan State Fair to import a pair of pandas for exhibition there, on the grounds that there was no substantial reason why the pandas should be brought into the country. Although the Michigan Department of Natural Resources had pledged their entire share of the revenues to the Chinese, the Fish and Wildlife Service decided that one of the uses to which this money might be put—to expanding the panda-breeding facility in Wolong—could actually harm the conservation effort (*New York Times*, 31 May 1988). Only a single cub has so far been bred at Wolong and the Fish and Wildlife service presumably concluded that with such an apparently poor record the damage inflicted by taking more animals from the wild was likely to outweigh the benefits that might accrue from the expansion of the breeding programme.

For the Chinese, already embarrassed over the Toledo incident, this was too much. On 16 September they announced that in view of the attitude of the US Fish and Wildlife Department, they would no longer be prepared to send pandas to the US (*New York Times*, 17 Sep. 1988). While zoos and conservationists continue discharging both barrels of their increasingly powerful political shotguns into their feet, it is unlikely that the Chinese will change this decision. This is unfortunate, since a properly controlled and managed loan system need not interfere with the captive-breeding programme, and as well as raising money would continue to publicise the conservation effort. The arrangements for the loan of London Zoo's Chia Chia to Cincinnati Zoo might serve as a model for such a system. Under the terms of this agreement, Chia Chia spent three months at Cincinnati in the autumn of 1988—with the consent of the US Fish and Wildlife Department—and the funds raised were used to finance the expansion of the panda-breeding facility at Mexico Zoo. Chia Chia has now been moved on to Mexico, where he will stay. It is hoped he will mate with Tohui, captive-bred daughter of Ying Ying and Pe Pe. There is also the possibility that Chia Chia could eventually also mate with the youngest cub, Chao Chao, whose sex is not yet known for certain although it is thought to be male. If this project proves unsuccessful, Chia Chia may move on to Tokyo and Washington.

Given the dangerously low numbers of pandas in the wild, few would disagree with the principle that using captive pandas to raise cash should not be allowed to interfere with the breeding programme. So far, that programme has met with only very limited success. Attempts to breed pandas in captivity in China began in 1955, but it was not until eight years later, on 9 September 1963, that Ming Ming, the first ever captive-bred giant panda, was born in Beijing Zoo. This historic event promised a new era of security for the species—at least in captivity. Li Li, the mother of Ming Ming, proved to be a model parent, cradling the cub in her arms day and night and responding to his every squeal. In September 1964 Li Li gave birth again, this time to a female named Lin Lin, and a year later a second female Chiao Chiao gave birth to the third Beijing cub, a male called Hua Hua.

For a while it appeared that many of the problems of breeding pandas in captivity must have been overcome, but detailed information was scarce outside China. Then in May 1966 the Red Guards appeared at Beijing University, and soon the country was in the grip of the cultural revolution. By 1977, 14 years after the birth of Ming Ming, only ten births had occurred at Beijing—six pairs of twins and four singletons. Of the 16 young, only seven had survived, and it was clear that optimism over the future of the panda in captivity was premature (Chin, 1979).

Western scientists had already discovered some of the problems for themselves. Even the fundamental task of sexing live pandas was proving to be embarrassingly difficult. The penis is normally hidden, and male giant pandas have no scrotum. The testes remain inside the body, and for most of the year they are inactive and reduced in size. Even during the breeding season the testes are protected by a thick layer of fat, so that except when the animal is stretched out on its back they do not produce a noticeable swelling. A reformed hunter I spoke to in Sichuan claimed to be able to distinguish males and females by the shape of their heads and shoulders, and keepers at Beijing Zoo say that females are gentler, more sociable, and have better, finer, cleaner-looking fur (Morris and Morris, 1966). There is no reason to doubt these claims, but even now Western biologists simply do not have enough experience of close contact with a range of animals to pick out such subtle differences. They are in the same position as a novice punter at a race-track to whom all thoroughbred horses look the same. It takes years of experience to spot a winner.

The earliest would-be panda breeders lacked even these elusive pointers. Having never seen a male panda, the staff of Brookfield Zoo were in no doubt at all that Su Lin was female. When Ruth Harkness left America on her second expedition to China in order to find a mate for Su Lin, her intent was to capture a young male. Although she found two cubs, both were apparently females. She returned to Chicago in February 1938 with one of them, Diana—later renamed Mei Mei. Six weeks later all hopes of mating Su Lin ended with her death.

The autopsy on Su Lin revealed that she was actually a male, but despite the doubts this must have raised the zoo continued to try to obtain a male as a mate for Mei Mei. But again males were apparently not to be found, and like Mei Mei, Mei Lan was thought to be female. Both eventually turned out to be males, so that all three pandas received in the West by the summer of 1938 were allocated to the wrong sex.

Tangier Smith achieved a much better record in sexing the five animals he brought from China to London, although in fairness to the American zoos it should be remembered that with the exception of Ming, these were more mature than any of the American animals and were consequently easier to sex. Four out of five were correctly identified, with only the unfortunate Dopey, renamed Sung, being mistaken for a female. This at least explained why he had shown no enthusiasm about mating with Tang.

With growing experience the record improved, although mistakes continued to be made. Pan Dee and Pan Dah at the Bronx Zoo were thought to be male and female respectively, but at autopsy both turned out to be females (Anon., 1945). As late as 1963 there were doubts about the sex of Chi Chi until she was examined under anaesthetic while undergoing treatment of an eye condition. With hindsight, the long series of errors proved to be totally irrelevant because it is unlikely that any of the pairs were capable of breeding. The only pair to reach maturity together were Happy and Pao Pei in St Louis Zoo. There are no records of attempts to breed the pair, but at his death in 1946 Happy showed signs of arterio-sclerosis and senility, indicating that he was almost certainly much older than first thought on his arrival at the zoo. By the time Pao Pei reached maturity— probably in 1944 or 1945—Happy was most likely past breeding age (S. Bircher, pers. comm.).

Even when the prospective partners were correctly identified as belonging to opposite sexes, breeding pandas proved to be less than straightforward. In 1966, in the middle of the decade of sexual liberation and beneath a blaze of television lights, Chi Chi and An An began to lay the foundations of a legend. Chi Chi had been caught in the wild in December 1957 as a very young cub and taken to Beijing Zoo. Here she remained until April of 1958, when she passed into the hands of Heini Demmer, an Austrian animal dealer. Demmer knew that Beijing was desperate to rebuild its collection and had offered to take Chi Chi in exchange for a collection of African game animals (Demmer, 1958a,b). She stopped briefly at Moscow Zoo, and spent some time in zoos in both East and West Berlin. Like so many famous pandas before her she was destined for Chicago, but at the last minute the US Treasury Department forbad her importation on the grounds that America did not recognise Communist China and was operating a trade embargo against the country under the 'Trading With the Enemy Act'. Eventually, she found her way to London, where she charmed the crowds as only a young playful panda can, and effectively gave the zoo no alternative but to buy her (Brambell, 1974).

In 1960 Chi Chi began showing signs of oestrus, but enquiries to Beijing about a possible mate were met with polite refusal. Then in 1964 the possibility was raised of attempting to mate her with Moscow Zoo's male, An An. An An had been given to Moscow in 1959 as a symbol of Sino–Soviet friendship, and after long negotiations Chi Chi was flown to Moscow and introduced to her prospective mate on 26 March 1966. After five days in adjacent enclosures, the two animals were put together, but almost immediately they began fighting and had to be separated. Chi Chi never came into heat, and the mating attempt was postponed until the autumn. In early October Chi Chi went off her food, and began presenting to her keeper. The normally silent An An had started to bleat, suggesting that he too was interested in mating. With the benefit of hindsight, it is unfortunate that the two animals were not introduced to each other immediately, because presenting behaviour is now known to be a sign of peak oestrus (Murata *et al.*, 1986) but by the time the political arrangements were finally completed and the animals were put together three days later her brief period of peak sexual receptivity had probably passed. An An was still enthusiastic, but Chi Chi rebuffed his advances with swipes and barks.

Chi Chi was flown back to London in October 1966. In the hope that she might be more receptive in familiar surroundings, London Zoo asked Moscow if they would agree to send An An to London for a further mating attempt. The meeting eventually took place in September, but once again Chi Chi showed no signs of oestrus, and even when artificially stimulated with hormone injections remained unreceptive. An An was allowed to remain at London Zoo until the spring of 1969, but again the endeavour proved futile. This time it seems likely that the autumn gonadotrophin injections had delayed Chi Chi's spring oestrus, and further injections failed to have the desired effect.

The prolonged saga of Chi Chi and An An gripped the attention of the media, and highlighted the difficulties in breeding captive pandas. Despite her oestrus behaviour, Chi Chi appeared more interested in soliciting the attentions of her human keepers than in mating with her own species. Taken from the wild as a young cub, she had never socialised with other pandas and had probably either not learned or had forgotten the responses appropriate to a female meeting a strange male. Faced with her confused reactions, An An performed remarkably well but was finally unable to overcome her resistance. Added to this were the problems ironically created by the animals' very value and scarcity. Artificial insemination was considered, but rejected because it would have involved anaesthetising An An to collect sperm, a risk that the London Zoo was not prepared to take. Had An An been less valuable and consequently been allowed to stay indefinitely in London, the hormone injections would probably not have been attempted and the outcome the following spring might have been different.

Subsequent experience has shown that very few males are capable of breeding in captivity. After the failure of the encounter between Chi Chi and An An there was still hope that this might be an exception and that other pandas would prove easier to handle. For several years it seemed that no-one outside China would get the opportunity to find out. Then in 1972 Chairman Mao Zedong made a gift of two pandas to the National Zoo in Washington to mark the visit to his country by former President Richard Nixon. Hsing Hsing, a male of about 18 months old, and Ling Ling, a female of perhaps two and a half years, arrived in America in April 1972 to begin a new era of breeding disasters.

The pair were kept in separate quarters from the day of their arrival in Washington, but were able to smell, hear and see each other through doors between their cages and through gaps in the dividing wall between their outdoor enclosures. On 26 May 1973 the keepers noticed that the two animals were becoming unusually interested in each other, and on that day and the next they were introduced and allowed to play together for several hours. Hsing Hsing mounted briefly several times, and Ling Ling adopted the receptive lordosis position with her tail raised, but at this stage it is almost certain that both animals were still immature. For the next seven years, whenever Ling Ling came into heat, the same story was repeated, with minor variations, but Hsing Hsing never succeeded in mating.

Although he had been kept in Beijing for several weeks after being given to the Nixons specifically in order to watch other animals mate, Hsing Hsing never quite got the idea and developed what has been euphemistically called an 'orientation problem'.

With Hsing Hsing apparently unable to cope with his responsibilities, an attempt was made to artificially inseminate Ling Ling in 1980. No pregnancy resulted, and so the London Zoo male, Chia Chia, was flown to Washington in March 1981 but the pair proved incompatible. Although Ling Ling was receptive, Chia Chia attacked and wounded her. In 1982 Hsing Hsing was reinstated as the prospective father, but when he failed to mate again, Ling Ling was anaesthetised and artificially inseminated with sperm from Chia Chia. Once again the procedure was a failure.

Eventually after seven years of unsuccessful encounters, the pair finally mated naturally on Friday 18 March 1983. To try to improve the chances of fertilisation, Ling Ling was anaesthetised the next day and again inseminated with sperm from the London Zoo male. The insemination was repeated the following day, and her adoring fans then settled down to watch and wait. Urinalysis suggested that Ling Ling might at last be pregnant, and in July she began gathering bamboo to make a 'nest' in her cage and finally gave birth to a 136 g male cub. Celebrations were brief, for the cub died only three hours later of a chest infection contracted in the womb.

After so many disappointments it must have been difficult for the zoo staff to draw any consolation from the biochemical studies on the cub's tissues that showed Hsing Hsing to be the father, even though this promoted him to the very select group of males proven capable of natural mating in captivity. Ling Ling then fell ill with a kidney infection, and although she recovered in time for another natural mating in 1984, the cub was stillborn.

In June 1987 Ling Ling again gave birth, this time to a pair of cubs. The first died almost immediately, and once again the surviving cub lasted only four days before succumbing to a bacterial infection. In April 1988 the pair mated yet again, three times in three consecutive days, but although there were encouraging signs Ling Ling failed to give birth.

Hopes were renewed at the National Zoo in Washington DC, when on 1 September 1989 the ageing Ling Ling gave birth to her fifth cub. The 113 g cub's first energetic squeals initially led zoo observers to believe they had finally achieved success with a healthy youngster. However, when veterinarians retrieved the cub from Ling Ling a day later and injected it with an immunising serum from father Hsing Hsing, they discovered the tiny pink-and-white panda was already suffering from an infection. After placing the cub in an incubator and transporting it to the zoo hospital, a team of veterinarians, assisted by nurses and pediatricians, worked around the clock to save the cub, which finally succumbed after a life of just 40 hours. This time, the cause of death was found to be an intestinal infection contracted from the mother's reproductive tract. The post mortem also revealed that the cub was a male and not a female as had originally been announced. Visitors to the zoo, who had been eagerly crowding into the Education Building to view Ling Ling and her cub by television monitor, found posted signs with the sombre announcement of the cub's death. The quest to breed the first panda in the United States continues, but Ling Ling is now probably close to the end of her reproductive life. However, Beijing Zoo's Li Li, mother of the world's first captive-born cub, had an oestrus period when she must have been at least 25 years of age, and so there is still a chance that in the next few years Li Li will eventually succeed in raising a cub of her own.

As well as the famous failures, there have also been some notable successes. First among these must be Chengdu Zoo's Mei Mei, the 17-year-old mother of seven cubs, all of which have survived infancy (UPI, 25 Sep. 1987). Mei Mei is clearly an exceptional mother, and only one of the five cubs born to other females at Chengdu has reached maturity. Arguably Beijing has an even better record, with 15 surviving cubs from 22 litters born to seven different females (Liu, 1988). Chongqing Zoo has three surviving cubs from five births, and Shanghai and Fuzhou one each. A single cub has also been born at the panda-breeding facility in Wolong. Kunming, Xian and Hangzhou have had nine births between them, but all the cubs have died young. In all, at the end of 1986 Chinese zoos could claim that 31 cubs born in captivity either reached maturity or were surviving at the time from a total of 49 litters—28 cases of twins, 20 singleton births, and one set of triplets (at Shanghai), making a total of 79 animals.

It is difficult to put these figures into perspective. In 1985 there were thought to be 67 pandas in Chinese zoos (Bertram and Gore, 1985) and present estimates of the number of giant pandas in captivity in China vary between 50 and 100, with 80 being the most often quoted figure. As well as the main collections at Beijing, Chengdu and Wolong and the animals in the zoos mentioned above, pandas have also been kept at various times at many other sites, and in a country the size of China it is especially difficult for outsiders to keep track of these. There are records of pandas in zoos at Tsing Tao, Lan Chou, Changsha, Guangzhou, Kuoming and Nanking, and two have become circus animals—one with the Shanghai Acrobatic Troupe and one with the Great Circus of China. Some of the animals in captivity are old, taken from the wild during the panda rescue programme, and are unlikely to breed, and others have yet to reach maturity. More importantly, no-one outside China knows how many animals have died in captivity. It is a reasonable guess that any zoo with a successful breeding programme must have high standards of management, and in these facilities there are probably few deaths that are a consequence of captivity. While accurate figures are impossible to obtain, it is generally accepted that between a quarter and a third of the adults in captivity in China produce offspring (Moore *et al.*, 1984), but much more information will be needed before a thorough assessment can be made of the Chinese breeding programme.

Outside China the situation is much clearer. In total, seven females have reached breeding age in captivity since the 1940s. Four of these have given birth to a total of 15 cubs, of which six are still alive. One of the most successful breeding programmes outside China has been at Mexico City's Chapultepec Zoo, which accounts for seven of these births. On 11 August 1980 Chapultepec became the first zoo outside China to witness the birth of a baby panda. The cub was named Xeng Li, but her inexperienced mother, Ying Ying, accidentally rolled over and crushed her only eight days later. In July 1981 Ying Ying gave birth to a second cub, a female named Tohui who became the first captive-born animal to survive infancy outside China. In March 1983 Ying Ying again came into oestrus, Tohui having been taken from her in December 1982, and although she seemed not to be in full heat, and aggressive towards Pe Pe, she mated again. This time the gestation period was much shorter than usual, and the zoo were shocked when she gave birth a month earlier than they were expecting, on 22 June. This third cub, Liang Liang, is still living, as are Xiu Hua, born in June 1985, and Chao Chao, born in June 1987. Tohui is now approaching breeding age, and it must be hoped that she will follow in her mother's footsteps, for Ying Ying died—reportedly of a heart attack—in January 1989.

In Tokyo the female, Huan Huan, presented to the Japanese in 1980, and her mate Fei Fei, who arrived two years later, have been the parents of three cubs. As frequently happens with many animals in captivity, the first of these died, but the second, Dong Dong, is still living, as is You You, born in June 1988.

The first cubs conceived by artificial insemination outside China were born in 1982 to Shao Shao in Madrid Zoo. She and her partner Chang Chang arrived in Madrid on Christmas Day 1978, aged 3 and 5 years old respectively, but although Shao Shao came into heat in 1979 and again in 1980 and Chang Chang showed interest, no mating occurred. When the animals once again failed to copulate in 1981 it was decided that hormone therapy and artificial insemination would be attempted the following year. In 1982 Chang Chang was injected with androgens, but although he attempted to mate at least nine times, he was unsuccessful. In less than 24 hours a team had flown to Madrid with semen from the London Zoo's male, Chia Chia, and after a hold-up by quite excusably incredulous customs officers at Madrid airport, Shao Shao was inseminated. Two cubs were born in September, but one was neglected by the mother and died three days later after attempts to hand-rear it failed. The other, a male named Chu Lin, is still surviving.

Artificial insemination has so far produced only three litters outside China, the other two being the cubs born to Huan Huan in Japan. This is a surprisingly low rate of success, for in theory at least the technique is not difficult. The male is anaesthetised, and in an undignified but painless operation, an electrode is inserted into the animal's rectum. A series of up to six brief shocks (less than 6 volts) is passed through the electrode to achieve erection. The electrode is then withdrawn slightly and the train of shocks repeated to stimulate ejaculation. The semen collected can then be checked for signs of infertility, and either used immediately or stored in liquid nitrogen.

The operation to inseminate the female is only slightly more difficult. The female is anaesthetised, and the semen introduced into the vagina using a catheter, the only real challenge being to guide the catheter past the obstructing ridges of the vaginal wall so that the semen can be deposited at the entrance to the cervix. In some species, the success of artificial insemination has been improved by injecting the semen directly into the uterus, but so far this has only occasionally been possible in the panda because the entrance to the cervix is very narrow. New equipment will in future allow semen to be introduced deep into the cervical canal or even into the uterus itself, but it is unlikly that this alone will make very much difference to the success-rate of artificial fertilisation because the main difficulties associated with the technique lie elsewhere.

As discussed in Chapter 4, male and female pandas in the wild spend several days or even weeks in the same area before mating, during which time the male is aware of the female's condition from her behaviour and the smell of her urine and her scent-marks. The female is receptive only for a very brief period, and it is the difficulty of predicting this period accurately in captivity that has been one of the most serious impediments to the success of artificial insemination. In captivity, females coming into oestrus go off their food, become restless, scent-mark more often, and begin to bleat— a call sounding very much like that of a goat and rarely heard at other times. As peak oestrus approaches, the female may present to the male or to her keepers, and will often rub her genital region with her fore-paw, but in the absence of a male giant panda there is no external sign which clearly signals that peak oestrus has actually arrived, and that the female has ovulated and could be fertilised. Consequently, the timing of artificial insemination was largely a matter of educated guesswork until a technique could be developed to determine the changes in hormone levels in the animal's urine.

The development of the technique of urinalysis and its subsequent refinement has allowed researchers to carry out artificial insemination with much greater confidence (Bonney et al., 1982; Moore et al., 1984). As in cats, dogs and humans it has been found that during the period leading up to oestrus, the urinary level of oestrogens increases steadily. This triggers a surge in luteinising hormone which in turn stimulates rupture of the ovarian follicle and release of the egg. If a female is housed with a male, the peak period of sexual interaction occurs immediately after the peak in oestrogen levels is reached, and the fall in oestrogen levels in the urine is therefore the most reliable guide to the timing of artificial insemination.

Even with the help of hormone assays, veterinarians still seem to be much less efficient than male pandas at fertilising females, and only time will tell whether this is due to lack of experience or a consequence of the panda's physiology. It is not impossible that the interaction of male and female before ovulation might affect the female's hormone levels in a way that facilitates fertilisation.

As well as the difficulty in getting giant pandas to conceive in captivity the problems of captive breeding are compounded by the high level of infant mortality. Only 39 per cent of the Chinese and 40 per cent of the non-Chinese captive-born cubs have survived infancy, compared for example with an average of 83 per cent for the brown bear and 78 per cent for the black bear. In part this can be attributed to the extreme helplessness of the young, although a primary cause of these figures is the inability of the mother to look after two young when twins are born. Only 16 animals from 58 born in captivity by 1986 as twins or triplets have survived to date (26 per cent), and a major improvement in the survival rate of new-borns could be achieved if the rejected cub in twin pregnancies could be reared by hand. All attempts at hand rearing have so far failed, but there has been little progress towards introducing a co-ordinated programme of research. An attempt was made to hand-rear one of the twins born at Madrid in 1982, keeping the cub in an incubator to prevent heat loss from the tiny and almost naked body. Sadly the cub died after four days from a sudden bacterial infection.

To develop a technique for the hand-rearing of giant pandas will not be easy. For the first few days of its life the cub will lie quietly only if it is gripped firmly by the mother. A hand-reared cub will need to be held constantly if it is not to be quickly exhausted by its own struggles. In China some cubs that have been hand reared have survived only a few hours, but others have lived for up to 45 days and reached weights of 1.4 kg. These cubs may have eventually died as a result of being fed an inappropriate diet of cow's milk. The few studies that have been carried out to date suggest that the milk of the panda is rather unusual, with very little sugar (Lyster, 1976; Hudson et al., 1984), although these data must be treated with caution since they are not the result of repeated sampling, and the composition of milk from many carnivores changes considerably as lactation progresses (Oftedal and Gittleman, 1989). Giant panda milk may be similar enough to the milk of the American black bear for diluted bear milk to be used as a substitute. Volunteers to milk female black bears are scarce, but milk could be obtained from hormone-treated anaesthetised animals. Alternatively, and more practically, suitable milk might be synthesised. The first few weeks would be difficult, but a cub that survived the early neonatal period would have a reasonable chance of reaching maturity, since we know from the experience with Su Lin that month-old cubs can be hand reared successfully.

If a successful captive-breeding programme can be established, it might conceivably serve one of three functions. The most modest scheme would be to establish a self-sustaining captive population. This is not impossible, since there is no single, insoluble problem that stands in the way of successful captive breeding. Rather, there are a series of difficulties—a naturally low rate of reproduction, aggravated by problems with getting the animals to conceive, and an unusually high level of neonatal mortality. With the major improvements in breeding success that could conceivably come about through hand-rearing, with improvements in artificial-insemination techniques and with the establishment of sperm banks to preserve genetic variety, this limited objective might well be achievable. However, there are many who feel that if the only objective of a captive-breeding programme is to secure the animal's future in captivity, then it is not a worthwhile exercise. A panda in a zoo, framed in the confines of its cage, lacks in itself the essence of a wild animal. To allow us to suspend our disbelief and imagine this animal in the wild, the illusion of freedom in the cage must be replaced by an idea of freedom inside our heads. If we know that the animal we are watching can never be free in the wild, the trick does not work and the animal is diminished. No longer a creature of the wild, it is a performing pet.

Valid though it may be, this argument is largely irrelevant since there is at least the possibility that captive-bred animals might one day be re-introduced to the wild. This raises the prospect of two additional, more ambitious functions for the captive-breeding programme: to supplement wild populations or to restock suitable habitat in which pandas are now extinct. Since there is a substantial captive population of pandas and the wild population is already at a critically low level, it would be foolish not to consider these possibilities carefully.

There have already been several cases where other species of animal have been successfully re-introduced into the wild. One such project already under way in China is the re-introduction of Père David's deer. By 1910 only a single female survived in China, but fortunately a captive population had already been established in Europe and was breeding well. A small herd was maintained on the Duke of Bedford's estate at Woburn, and in 1956 two pairs were sent to Beijing. In 1957 the first calf was born there and two small herds are now happily re-established, one in a park near Beijing and the other in a 1,000-ha enclosure in Jiangsu province.

It is arguable that these animals are still not truly wild. Inside their enclosures they are protected from predators, and their environment is not substantially different from that in which the herd has been maintained in 'captivity' for hundreds of years. The re-introduction of the Arabian oryx into Oman provides a more realistic demonstration of the possibilities and pitfalls of such a programme. Between 1980 and 1984 17 animals from zoos in the United States and one from Jordan were shipped to Oman and held in pens before release into a larger enclosure of 100 ha. Here a herd was kept under observation until a stable social structure had developed before the animals were released into the main re-introduction area, a reserve of 25,000 km². By carefully planning the release of the oryx and allowing a cohesive herd to develop in the larger enclosure, the biologists have managed to encourage the development of a functional social structure before exposing the animals to the harsh conditions of the desert. Consequently, the animals have successfully made the physical, physiological and behavioural adjustments necessary to lead an independent existence in their native habitat (Price, 1986).

Whether captive-bred pandas could adapt to life in the wild is uncertain, for not all release programmes have been so successful. Zoo-bred animals that have not had social contact with others at crucial stages in their development may be unable to associate normally with wild animals, a problem that was at least partly responsible for the failure of the programme to re-introduce the bald ibis in Turkey (Burgman *et al.*, 1988). The ibis could not feed themselves in the wild, behaviour that would normally have been learned from their parents. Consequently the population never became established in the wild and they remained dependent on humans.

We know far too little about pandas to even guess at how growing up in captivity might affect the development of their foraging or their reproductive behaviour. Beyond the fundamental uncertainty about the ability of captives to survive at all in the wild and to integrate themselves into a natural population, are other essential questions that as yet remain unanswered. At present it is normal practice to remove a cub from its mother in time to bring her into oestrus the following season so that she can mate again. This might in theory double her reproductive rate, but does it affect the cub's ability to socialise with other pandas? Are captive-reared cubs more likely to mate as adults if released into habitat that already has an established population, or would the best strategy be to release groups of captives into virgin, unpopulated habitat? Answering these questions will pose formidable problems, and at present there are so few zoo-reared cubs that they are largely irrelevant. But if the captive-breeding programme is to do more than produce exhibits for zoos, they are questions that must soon be answered.

Not all the problems encountered in the release of captive-bred animals necessarily apply to pandas. The differential birth and survival of animals adapted to breeding in captivity can alter the genetic composition of the captive population making captive-bred animals genetically incompatible with wild animals. This is very unlikely to be relevant to the conservation of the panda because the animals are long-lived and breed slowly. Ten generations from now, in the middle of the next century, it seems likely that the gene pools will have changed little, and if the panda is not securely protected by then it will almost certainly be extinct in the wild.

The captive breeding of red pandas raises a rather different set of problems. Although red pandas are much easier to keep in captivity than giant pandas, they do not thrive in traditional small mammal enclosures and cannot cope with extremes of heat or humidity. They are susceptible to disease, in particular to canine distemper virus, and several captive animals have been inadvertently killed by injections of modified live virus vaccines intended to inoculate them against the disease (Bush and Roberts, 1977). A paper published in the first edition of *The Red or Lesser Panda Studbook* in 1980 concluded on the basis of computer predictions that the captive population was destined for extinction (Veeke and Glatston, 1980), but over the last ten years there has been a marked improvement in the success of captive-breeding programmes due to improvements in housing and health care, and the outlook is now more optimistic. The current captive population is still small, and as a whole is growing only slowly, but the growth of the North American population over the past few years shows what can be achieved (Glatston and Roberts, 1988). Notably, 79 young were born at Washington Zoo between 1972 and 1982, and during this time the captive population increased from two to over 50 animals, including twelve breeding pairs (Roberts, 1982). Not that there is cause for complacency; many of these animals are not breeding, and since the entire captive population is derived from only 27 individuals, many pairs are producing inbred young (Princée, 1988).

One reason why this has been possible is that like giant pandas, red pandas often give birth to twins, but unlike giant pandas they are able to rear both offspring. Red pandas occasionally give birth to triplets or even quads. It is rare that all the young in these larger litters survive if left with the mother, but young from these large litters have been successfully cross-fostered to other mothers that have lost their young, or reared by hand.

18. In captivity, giant pandas usually sniff at each bamboo shoot before they eat it. The smell may provide clues about the nutritional value of the plant. In the wild, pandas are very choosy about their food, often selecting only a few stems from the dozens that may be within their reach. (WWF/Timm Rautert)

19. A tranquillised captive is carried to suitable habitat where it will be released back into the wild. Trapping and relocation may become important in future giant panda management if the harmful consequences of inbreeding are to be avoided. *(Ken Johnson)*

Young that failed to gain weight as expected have also been reared successfully by supplementing their diet with artificial milk while keeping them with the mother. This system is generally preferable to complete hand-rearing, which has had mixed success and denies the cubs the chance of learning social behaviour from their mother. On average, 60 per cent of cubs born at Washington survived to maturity (three years old).

In January 1988 a total of 243 red pandas were registered with the *Red Panda Studbook* as part of the international captive-breeding programme. Of these, 86 belong to the Chinese subspecies, *Ailurus fulgens styani* or Styan's panda (Glatston, pers. comm.). When planning a captive-breeding programme, it is often difficult to know how to treat a subspecies like Styan's panda. Are the differences between the two subspecies sufficient to warrant maintaining them as two separate zoo populations, or would it be better to treat them as a single species and interbreed, so increasing the genetic diversity of the captive population? The question becomes particularly significant when, as in the case of Styan's panda, the number of captive animals is close to the critical figure at which problems from inbreeding might be expected. Miles Roberts, a leading authority on the red panda in captivity, has re-examined the characters used to distinguish the two subspecies and found insufficient significant differences to justify their separation (Roberts, 1982a). This is always a matter for argument, since there is no clear-cut dividing line between two subspecies, and a basic criterion of classification is that a subspecies is 'good' when enough taxonomists agree on it. He suggested that the original red panda described by F. W. Styan may just have been unusually large, and that the two 'subspecies' should perhaps be treated as a single species and interbred. This would certainly have reduced the risk of inbreeding in the red panda population as a whole. But biochemical tests on blood samples taken from both subspecies have since shown that there are enough genetic differences between the two to warrant maintaining each as a separate population (Roberts, 1987; Gentz, 1987).

The chances of creating a viable population of Styan's panda in captivity outside China have improved considerably over the last few years, due partly to the registration of pandas in Japanese zoos, most of which are *A.f. styani*, and partly to China's new wave of 'panda diplomacy' using red pandas. The use of more sophisticated management techniques, the consequent improvements in the success of captive breeding, and the free exchange of animals between zoos as part of a co-ordinated breeding programme should ensure the future of the subspecies in captivity for many years to come.

It is now possible to be cautiously optimistic about the prospects for the captive population of red pandas. By contrast, the captive-breeding programme for giant pandas seems to be faced with a mountain of problems. Although each of these is probably soluble given enough time, for the giant panda time is running out. Roughly 10 per cent of the population is already in captivity. At present, captive breeding cannot even maintain a self-sufficient captive population. Recently there has been a marked improvement in the level of dialogue and co-operation between Western and Chinese zoos. Towards the end of 1988 Chinese zoos agreed to set up a studbook and work out a detailed breeding plan (*Independent*, 21 Feb. 1989). This necessitates moving animals between zoos to maximise the chances of success, something which has proved difficult in the past. By pooling their shared expertise, Chinese and Western zoologists may succeed in reaching their newly declared goal—a stable captive population. Even if they do, the possibility of successfully releasing pandas bred in captivity into the wild is uncertain.

Re-introduction cannot possibly succeed unless the original reasons for the panda's extinction are removed. A re-introduction programme would take more planning, require more political support and be more expensive than a proper programme of protection. With present levels of expertise in captive breeding, the only certain hope of a secure future for the giant panda lies in ensuring adequate protection of the wild population.

6. Conservation

On 17 October 1981 Britain's most prestigious newspaper printed a short but controversial article entitled 'Zoo accused of waste in breeding Pandas'.

We can quite easily save the pandas [*The Times* assured its readers] but what is the point if they are evolutionary dead ends? The species is a fairly good example of a 'post pleistocene relic' [*sic*], that is, one of a group of survivors of the last ice age that has been slowly dying off as their habitats contracted naturally. Another example is the North American buffalo.

It is true that the panda is a survivor from before the last ice-age, but it is a nonsense to suggest that a relict species is automatically either rare or doomed. The North American buffalo probably numbered more than 60 million animals before the appearance of man, and even in 1871 the population was estimated at more than 12 million. By 1890 their numbers had fallen to an estimated 1,000 animals, not because they were a maladapted relict of the Pleistocene era, but because people killed them.

The research work which was just beginning in China as this article appeared has also uncovered very little evidence that the giant panda's steady demise is the result of its 'notorious sexual and thus procreative inefficiency' and 'general unfitness for survival', to quote another *Times* article a few months later. Far from being poorly adapted to its naturally shrinking habitat, it shows both the giant and red pandas to be an integral part of a complex and thriving ecosystem. What threatens the panda is not its evolutionary history, its reproductive system or its peculiar choice of food: it is trapping and the destruction of its habitat by people.

Who will look tomorrow's children in the eye and tell them we allowed the pandas to die? Endless reasons have been proposed to explain the demise of the giant panda, as if to prepare the world for its eventual extinction and excuse ourselves from all blame. It is not only journalists who take this view. Scientific journals are scattered with papers announcing that the giant panda is doomed by its Stone-age size, or its over-specialised diet, or the natural contraction of its range through climatic changes. To make it easier for ourselves, we have tried to convince each other that when these wonderful beasts finally become extinct it will have been their fault and not ours. It has even been argued that the giant panda is unable to reproduce efficiently because of the unusual protrusions on the head of its sperm. Unfortunately for this last theory, the only other mammal with similar sperm is the degu, a small rodent from South America. One of the commonest mammals in central Chile, it regularly gives birth to litters of ten young.

In recent years conservation has become an increasingly important issue on the political agenda, but the outlook for most rare and endangered mammals is dismal. In the West politicians and governments still show a predictable preference to involve themselves in gestures that promise a quick return. In October 1988 over a million dollars could be found to free three grey whales trapped in ice near Barrow in Alaska. But even in the rich industrialised countries, money for long-term and less spectacular projects is always in short supply. Faced with the need to feed burgeoning human populations, pressure from multi-national mining and timber companies and ruthless poachers chasing the vast profits to be made from ivory, horn and skins, poorer countries can rarely afford the cost of effective conservation, whatever their sympathies. Non-governmental organisations working within these countries often find themselves unable to criticise their hosts and reluctant to admit to those who provide their funds that the measures being adopted are inadequate.

As for almost all other endangered animals, the main threat to the survival of the red and giant pandas is the destruction of their habitat. Throughout their range, the story is much the same. Farmers hungry for land push ever higher up the mountain slopes, felling trees for fuel and building materials, and cutting the new growth for animal fodder. At an altitude of 4,000 m trees are slow to recover, and even without the pressures of cutting and grazing may take 80 or 90 years to reach a diameter of 20–25 cm. In practice these pressures are relentless. Cattle, sheep and goats graze any emerging seedlings and prevent regeneration of the forest, and their hooves loosen the thin mountain soil. With no protective tree cover, the summer rains scour the mountainsides, causing landslides and erosion that wash the topsoil into the streams and rivers. The water-holding capacity of the soil is reduced, and in the dry season the streams disappear. The situation is perhaps worst in Nepal, where 50 per cent of the country's forest cover has been lost in the last decade and the human population, estimated in 1973 to be over 11 million, is doubling every 30 years. In some areas women must now work all day just to collect a head-load of sticks for firewood. An estimated 10 million cattle and 4.5 million sheep compete with wildlife for the little fodder that remains.

In the 1988 *Red List* the red panda is still listed as 'insufficiently known', meaning that it is probably vulnerable, rare or endangered but there is not enough information to decide which (IUCN, 1988). A conservation programme initiated by the Nepalese government in 1971 led to the passing of the National Parks and Wildlife Conservation Act in 1973, which provides the basis for the administration of protected areas. Nepal now has an extensive network of National parks, staffed by well-trained and dedicated local people who are succeeding in slowing the destruction by the parks' human inhabitants. In a country where the worst consequences of deforestation are already painfully obvious, it is relatively easy to persuade the population that the ecological wellbeing of the mountains is essential to the welfare of mountain and lowland communities alike. Yet there is little cause for optimism. Despite this protection, the mortality rate of red panda cubs in the Langtang National Park is over 80 per cent, and in 1986 only a single cub was born in an area of 35 km² under study by researchers from the University of Maine (Fleming, 1988). With cheap loans available for investment in livestock, and with government encouragement, local people are grazing increasing numbers of domestic animals in the park. Disturbed by cows, yaks and their human minders, female pandas will not return to their dens for fear of revealing their locations. Many young consequently die of thirst or starvation. The growing human population and shifts in traditional patterns of livelihood are putting increasing pressure on the mountains. In addition, the red panda's habitat in Nepal is now threatened by the rapidly growing demand for wood by tourists, trekkers and mountaineers.

In Bhutan, to the east of Nepal, the threats are much the same. Bhutan is a Buddhist kingdom that until recently was almost completely closed to outside influences. However, since the country joined the United Nations in 1972, the economy has been expanding, and a veneer and plywood factory at Gedhu has already severely depleted the surrounding forests. Large tracts of forest have also been cleared to provide grazing for herds of cattle, yak and dzo. The familiar cycle of deforestation and erosion has already begun. Ironically, the strict Buddhist culture which prevents the killing of animals is adding to the problem. Unproductive cattle are never culled, and farmers are forced to maintain larger herds than would be necessary to meet their physical needs. On the other hand, the Buddhist injunction against killing has spared most of the animals in Bhutan from the pressures of hunting, and although musk deer are taken for their scent glands by poachers from across the Indian border, most reports imply that wild animals are still abundant. The most serious threat to the habitat of the red panda in Bhutan may well be Western 'philanthropy' which as one observer points out 'has paid considerably more attention to helping with extraction than to coping with reafforestation and erosion' (Sargent, 1985).

In China the red panda is officially accorded complete protection (Glatston, 1980), but in reality its greatest security is a consequence of sharing its range with the giant panda. Nature reserves and the protection of wildlife are not the highest priorities of Chinese environmental policy. Not surprisingly, pollution control, reafforestation, watershed protection and birth control are considered to be the more urgent environmental issues. Although protection of the flora and fauna is only a small part of this overall programme, eventual success will be possible only if these other aspects of environmental protection are effective.

Contrary to popular belief, the Chinese do not have a culture that is particularly sympathetic to wild animals. It is often said that Oriental peoples regard wildlife as an integral part of nature to be respected and allowed to live in harmony with man. On the contrary, Chinese attitudes differ little from those of Westerners. Certain species have always been regarded as nuisances because they destroy crops, prey on domestic livestock or attack people; in the past they were even viewed as forces of evil and darkness (Shen *et al.*, 1982).

The giant panda is fortunate to be treated as a special case, and because it is rare, endemic to China, and world famous, its conservation is an issue that the Chinese authorities have always appeared to take seriously. As early as 1946 the Hong Kong newspaper *Da Gong Bao* warned that if panda hunting continued, the animal was likely to become extinct (*Da Gong Bao*, 1946). With the success of the revolution in 1949, the giant panda was declared a 'National Treasure' by the new Communist regime, and at the third National People's Congress in 1957, the Communist Party determined to set up forest reserves. In 1962 a resolution was passed by the State Council—the body responsible for the day-to-day running of the country— to ensure the 'positive protection and rational use of wild animal resources.'

(Giant Panda Expedition, 1974). The export of skins was banned, and the resolution stipulated that 'the giant panda is a rare and precious animal' and declared that nature reserves would be established for its protection (Zhu and Li, 1980).

As highly specialised animals with no close relatives, uniquely adapted to a dwindling habitat, pandas would be the logical recipients of an exceptional conservation effort even if they were not so enormously popular with the general public (Lang, 1977). In May 1980 a plan of action was drawn up by the Chinese Association for Environmental Sciences, the Ministry of Forestry, Academia Sinica and the World Wildlife Fund. A massive programme was agreed, which included the building of a research centre, jointly funded by the Ministry of Forestry and the World Wildlife Fund, in the Wolong Reserve in Sichuan. Research would be carried out on the ecology, population biology and food selection of free-living pandas, and on the management and breeding of captive animals (Schaller *et al.*, 1985).

The China/World Wildlife Fund project was the logical extension of the fledgling conservation programme already underway in China, which began in 1956 with the setting up of the Dinghu Mountain Preserve in Guangdong province. The twelve panda reserves now designated are estimated to protect rather more than half of the total panda population, but just how big that population actually is still defies accurate analysis. Between 1974 and 1976 about 3,000 Chinese scientists carried out the first intensive survey to determine the status of the giant panda in the wild, and estimated that between 1,000 and 1,100 animals remained (O'Brien and Knight, 1987). That population may now have dropped to between 600 and 700, according to the results of a census commissioned by the national Sichuan provincial and local forestry bureau in 1985. Other reports claim that the population in Wolong has also fallen to roughly half its 1976 level, from 145 animals then to 72 now (Schaller, 1987). For many reasons it is dangerous to take these figures too seriously. Most importantly, the 1970s survey was conducted using quite different techniques from those employed in the more recent study, and so the results are not directly comparable. This has not prevented considerable press speculation over the interpretation of the figures, but even if there has been a real decline in numbers since the mid-seventies, what does this actually tell us? Bamboo die-off does not have long-term effects on the population, but a 'weeding out' of old and sick animals during the mass flowering of the last few years would be expected even if the populations were totally undisturbed by man. Does a decrease in numbers reflect a real decline in the panda population, or is it just a temporary set-back? The numbers game makes good headlines, but it is a poor basis for a conservation strategy.

Whatever the number of pandas surviving in the wild, it is quite clear that the giant panda will become extinct in the next century unless more steps are taken to protect its habitat. According to a World Wildlife Fund news release in 1987 'Satellite images reveal that forest clearance for agriculture will be the main cause of panda extinction, not lack of food through bamboo flowering.' (WWF, 1987) Even in reserves where there is no more commercial logging, the loss of forest cover continues at a horrifying pace.

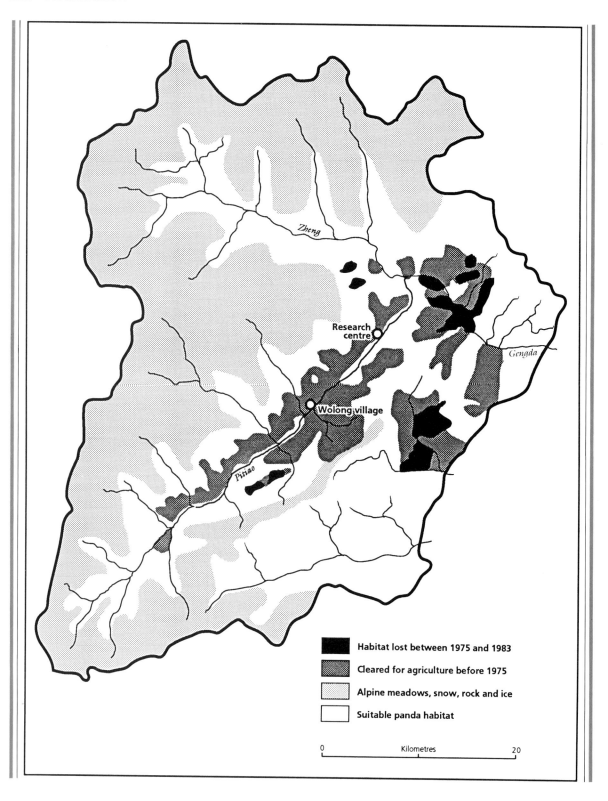

Habitat lost between 1975 and 1983

Cleared for agriculture before 1975

Alpine meadows, snow, rock and ice

Suitable panda habitat

0   Kilometres   20

Figure 20. Loss of panda habitat in the Wolong reserve since 1975.

In Wolong, peasants have destroyed 14 km² of forest between 1975 and 1983, and in other areas of panda range the situation is even more serious (De Wulf *et al.*, 1988).

In the last 30 years Sichuan has lost some 30 per cent of its forests, and more than half of the natural forest vegetation has been destroyed or disturbed so badly that it no longer provides suitable panda habitat. Pandas do not just need bamboo. They need large trees for scent-marking, and sheltered sites (often in huge hollow trees) for use as maternity dens. Clear-felling creates a habitat almost useless to giant pandas even though bamboo may continue to grow. It is not only pandas that face long-term difficulties if the forests are clear-felled. Valuable timber trees like fir and hemlock do not readily invade the clear-cut areas. Instead, they are replaced by birch and maple whose light, wind-borne seeds make them better colonisers (Taylor and Qin, 1989). Selective felling which left maturing fir and hemlock trees standing would be a more prudent method of timber extraction in the large area of panda habitat that at present falls outside the borders of reserves. As well as ensuring a future supply of valuable timber, selective felling would cause much less disturbance to the panda's habitat. Large conifers could be left as den sites, and the shade of the remaining trees would ensure that the bamboo under-storey could regenerate normally after flowering.

As well as the threat to its habitat, the panda is faced with other problems. Although the fur trade has long been of considerable value to the Chinese economy (in the first half of 1934 the sale of furs from China brought in over $US 23 million, more than either tea or silk) (*China Press*, 24 Oct. 1934), the panda has been little sought after by hunters until recently. Its fur is coarse and slightly oily, unsuitable material for the luxury-fur market. Chinese medicine has found no use for any part of the panda. Yet trappers have long been killing pandas by accident, in snares set for musk deer.

Musk deer are small, timid creatures that range across the Himalayas and the eastern edge of the Tibetan plateau through north-eastern China and into Siberia. Male musk deer have no antlers, but instead have long canine teeth that project below the upper lip. They also carry a scent gland, the pod, in a sac between their genitals. This produces a viscous, oily secretion, a base for expensive perfumes, and an ingredient of medicines used to treat a range of diseases from sore throats to rheumatism. In a single year Japan imported 5,000 kg of musk, which at a conservative estimate would have involved the trapping and killing of 350,000 musk deer. Not surprisingly, musk deer are becoming rare. The Himalayan population is now estimated at 30,000 animals, of which half may be killed annually (Green, 1986). As the animals become rarer, the price of musk goes up. A kilo may fetch $US 45,000, or three times the price of gold. Each pod contains roughly 25 g of musk—worth over $1,000. For people whose monthly wage is perhaps only $US 30 to $US 40, trapping musk deer is obviously an attractive sideline. As a result some pandas are also killed, strangled in the snares.

Accidental snaring and deliberate hunting are probably the main cause of the recent, sudden decline in panda numbers. In Wolong the 1974 census tallied 145 pandas; by 1986 there were only 72. Snaring is not a new

Figure 21. A male musk deer. Snares set for these animals are a major cause of panda mortality.

lem: in February 1936 Arthur Sowerby wrote in the Shanghai Newspaper *China Press* that snares being used to hunt musk deer were doing untold damage.

> One of the worst of these is the foot-noose, set in a runway and fastened to a bent-down sapling in such a way that when the animal puts its foot into the fatal ring and springs the trigger, the noose tightens on its foot and the sapling straightens up, yanking the wretched animal into the air where it hangs suspended by one leg until merciful death frees it from suffering. This inhuman trap is used in Sichuan by hunters of the musk deer. It is pointed out that it is brutal in the extreme and wanton and wasteful due to the fact that it catches female musk deer just as often as it catches the males and since females have no musk pods they are of no value. (*China Press*, 16 Feb. 1936)

Fifty years on it is no longer necessary to hoist the deer into a tree, since there are few leopards or bears left in the hills that might scavenge the carcass. Nothing else has changed, except of course that for both musk deer and pandas, extinction in the wild is now perilously close.

Musk deer are protected under CITES—the Convention on International Trade in Endangered Species—which China signed in 1980. However, trade in musk is not illegal, since an exception is made in the case of musk obtained from animals in captivity. Unfortunately, musk deer are nervous, solitary animals, and maintaining them in captivity, let alone breeding them, has proved extremely difficult. Musk from deer farms accounts for only a tiny percentage of the international trade, but provides a cover for widespread illegal trading.

Musk is only one of many products derived from animal and plant species that share the panda's range and which are thought by the Chinese to have healing properties. The remedies of traditional Chinese medicine have recently been exposed to medical testing and analysis in the West, and some have been found to be the source not just of new drugs but of whole new classes of drugs. If logging and agriculture are allowed to destroy the panda's habitat, then some of the plants that provide such drugs will undoubtedly be lost forever. The giant panda is important not only for its own sake but because it acts as an 'indicator species', the most sensitive inhabitant of its ecosystem to environmental degradation. Its demise sounds a warning, and it is certain that its extinction would quickly be followed by the loss of many other species. To squander such a rich genetic legacy would be an act of extreme foolishness.

Now the embattled pandas face a new threat. According to a *Sunday Times* report in August 1983, a Taiwanese company was offering skins for sale at $US 25,000 each, and conservationists called for strong action by the Chinese to stamp out the trade. Hunting of pandas had already been outlawed by the 1962 Act. In Wolong a farmer who accidentally trapped a panda in a snare set for musk deer had received a two-year jail sentence, but with such huge potential profits to be made, many peasants in remote areas must have been tempted. In October 1987 the Chinese Supreme Court warned that anyone found guilty of killing a giant panda or smuggling hides would be charged under criminal code regulations governing offences that damage the economy and treated as a serious criminal, risking a jail sentence of between 10 years and life, and possibly even the death penalty (UPI, 2 Oct. 1987). In February 1988 the first threat was carried out, and eleven people were given life sentences for killing two pandas.[1] It appears that these isolated cases are part of a trade in panda skins that may now be worth millions of dollars. In recent years the Chinese authorities have recovered 146 pelts. According to Gao Dezhan, China's Minister of Forestry, 203 arrests have been made, and a total of at least 26 people have now been sentenced to between one year and life imprisonment for attempting to smuggle skins out of the country. The main market for skins appears to be Japan, where they may be fetching as much as $US 200,000 dollars each (Anon., 1988).

Any attempt to reverse the decline in panda numbers is faced with many different problems. Fundamental to any hope of long-term success must be an attempt to educate everyone living in or near a panda habitat about the aims and objectives of the conservation effort. The Chinese government has begun to tackle this, and in 1986 a campaign was launched in 5,000 villages and forest farms throughout Sichuan, to teach farmers and villagers about panda protection, and to discourage the cutting of bamboo, as well as to give advice on how to cope with starving pandas (de Havilland, 1987). To prevent antipathy towards the project, local authorities in Sichuan allocated special funds to reimburse peasants whose homes or crops had been damaged by marauding pandas desperate for food after the bamboo flowered.

These are commendable measures, but to win the hearts and minds of the Chinese people to conservation will be an enormous task, which through Western eyes seems comparable to that facing Père David in his battle to convert them to Christianity. Much of the wildlife of China was until very recently seen as nothing more than a potential ingredient in Chinese medicine, and although the practical value of wildlife might eventually help convince pragmatists of the importance of conservation, that value is at present helping to drive many species to the brink of extinction. In a walk round the bustling medicinal market in Chengdu one afternoon we saw ibex and gazelle horns, antlers of sambar deer, shells of pangolins and turtles, monkeys paws, and the carcasses of more than 50 black bears. Pelts of rare animals were also openly offered for sale. We counted a dozen red panda skins, along with skins of two clouded leopards, several snow leopards, a common leopard, dhole, and several smaller cats. At one stall we stopped to take photographs, and were asked if we were reporters. After being reassured that we were only tourists, the owners placed a newspaper over a pile of snow leopard skins and let us snap away to our hearts' content. After a similar trip to the Taicheng outdoor market in Guangdong province, Orville Schell wrote

> A unique section of the market was a stretch of street where wild animals were sold, or what an American friend of mine came to call the 'gourmet meat section'. Here one could buy live owls, hawks, songbirds, rats, monkeys, lizards, frogs, snakes, badgers, weasels, wildcats, and assorted other exotic animals that can be profitably trapped and sold by Chinese peasants because many Chinese believe their ingestion bestows longevity or increases their virility. In fact so severe has the depletion of predators become that in March 1984, the Ministry of Forestry's wildlife protection department warned the country of a new problem: the rodent population was reaching dangerous proportions. These officials estimated that rodents annually destroyed 5,000,000 tons of grain, ruined large numbers of trees, and devoured millions of tons of fodder already in short supply. But if the Chinese of Taicheng market were concerned about, or even aware of such long-range problems, there was no evidence of it. As long as there was money to be made, wild animals would be sold. (Schell, 1985)

At the other end of the country the situation was until recently very much the same. According to a report in the Sept. 1987 issue of *Beijing Review*, dishes made from endangered animals could be found on the menus of 90 hotels and restaurants in Harbin, the capital of Heliongjiang province.

Many, perhaps all of the medicinal markets have recently been closed down, following the passage of a new Wildlife Act in China, but it is the contrast between the attitudes of a new generation of Chinese entrepreneurs, and the clear commitment of the Chinese government to try to save the giant panda from extinction that makes analysis of the prospects for success so difficult. Despite the obvious gap between the articulated conservation policy of the Chinese government and reality, the determination of the Chinese authorities should not be underestimated. The World Wildlife Fund (now the World Wide Fund for Nature) has contributed some $US 4 million toward panda conservation, including the capital cost of establishing the panda-breeding centre in Wolong, and have helped with money towards research and training. But the cost to China of these measures has also been considerable. Logging operations have stopped within the reserves, resulting in a loss of income from forestry. Buildings and roads constructed for the forestry operation are now deserted. In places whole plantations have been abandoned. Agriculture and grazing are restricted. In Wolong alone, the decision by the Ministry of Forestry to abandon logging operations in 1975 meant sacrificing a capital investment of close to $US 6 million, a figure that does not include the projected costs of lost revenue. When questioned about the decision, a senior forestry official answered simply, 'the giant panda is priceless' (Sitwell, 1977).

As well as accepting a loss of income from once profitable industries, the Chinese have made substantial contributions themselves. In a single year, 1984, the total bill for panda-rescue operations alone came to some $US 2 million (UPI, 27 Dec. 1984).

The cost of saving the panda is not only financial. China must feed over 1,000,000,000 people with the produce of just 15 per cent of the land they live on, and consequently it is a brave move to declare that people must give up orchards and fertile land for an animal. Despite determined attempts by the Chinese to limit population growth with a public awareness prog-ramme, backed up by financial penalties for any family raising more than a single child (and incentives for those who sign a single-child pledge), the population is still rising. Even if the policy of 'One couple—one child' can be maintained into the next century, the population will reach 1,200,000,000 by the year 2000, simply because there are so many young Chinese who have yet to begin raising a family. Yet even in the face of this overwhelming population growth, and subsequent pressure to increase food production, 300 people have been moved from farms inside the boundary of Tangjiahe reserve to villages lower down the valley, at a cost of 1.1 million Yuan ($US 367,000) (Machlis and Johnson, 1987).

Unfortunately, in a country of over 9 million km², with some 55 national minorities, such decisions are not always put into effect so easily. In June 1984 the Chinese authorities announced their intention to relocate 2,000 people from the heart of the Wolong Reserve to a less sensitive area, but only a few have left their homes and moved to the new houses built for them lower down the valley. There are no legal precedents in China for enforcing such a move, but part of the explanation for the tolerance that the Chinese government has displayed in accepting the failure of its plan may well be that the people concerned are not Han Chinese (who make up the bulk of the population of China), but are mostly members of an ethnic minority group, the Chiang. Separatist sentiments among minority groups have always endangered the stability of the Chinese state, and not wishing to incite trouble along its borders, China is generally indulgent towards its minorities. For example, in 1986, there were 14.7 million births in China, 1.6 million more than had been expected. Many of these 'extra' births occurred in remote rural areas among the ethnic minorities, where the rules on one child per family are interpreted rather more flexibly (*China Daily*, 2 Apr. 1987).

Most parts of eastern China have been under cultivation for thousands of years, and very little primary vegetation remains. The very areas of greatest interest to conservationists are the less fertile mountains and deserts, areas traditionally inhabited by ethnic minorities. Flexibility in the Chinese approach to birth control among these groups inevitably puts even greater human population pressure on these sensitive and as yet comparatively unspoilt areas, but thankfully the signs are that the policy towards birth control among minority groups is changing—an inevitable step perhaps, since the prospect of these historicaly troublesome people becoming majorities in the next century must appear alarming in Beijing.

How is it that in spite of the concerted campaign aimed at its protection, the area of panda habitat continues to decline? Even inside the reserves where the government has called a halt to commercial logging, deforestation continues. It is now a slow, insidious process. Forest guards employed to stop illegal felling are reluctant to act. When shown an area of forest that had been felled by local peasants, a guard in the Wolong Reserve retorted 'Yes, but the people need these trees for firewood.' It is difficult not to have some sympathy with his dilemma. Every man and woman in these valleys has spent a lifetime scratching a living from the stony mountain soil. Firewood, and timber for housing are not luxuries, and few can afford to buy them from legitimate sources. Wood is now in such short supply in China that since 1980 the free market price for a cubic metre of pine wood has gone up seven times, and now costs around $US 1,500. A Chinese grain farmer might hope to make this much profit in a year. In such a small, conservative community is it surprising that many guards, themselves often drawn from local villages, are unwilling to report timber cutting? Each individual who cuts a winter supply of fuel is involved in only a minor offence. Indeed, although the education programme discourages the cutting of trees, felling timber is not actually an offence unless the perpetrator is caught red-handed with more than 5 m³—an unlikely event.

As the demand for timber grows and the supply falls, the situation becomes even more desperate. According to Professor Luo Zhuchong of the Ministry of Forestry, 'Local people have been fighting and killing each other over forestry rights. Even the guards are shot' (*Guardian*, 7 Feb. 1989). This escalation of the conflict is hardly likely to encourage the already reluctant forest guards to tackle timber cutting seriously.

As if this alone were not enough, the panda will in future face another threat. As a result of the economic liberalisation under Deng Xiaoping, many urban Chinese are now getting their first taste of affluence, and a new tourist industry has been created. Joined by ever increasing numbers of visitors from Hong Kong and Macau, many tourists are now heading for the scenic beauty of western Sichuan. So far, only Jiuzhaigou has been seriously affected. The long string of glacial lakes that wind through the valley bottoms cascading into each other over spectacular waterfalls, make this the most beautiful of the panda reserves. But along with jobs and much needed income, tourism has brought hotels, cars, buses, trails, waste-disposal problems and habitat disturbance. It may not be long before cable-cars take tourists high up the mountains and into the heart of the little area of panda habitat that remains. Soon other reserves may face similar problems. Tourism can be an important ally of conservation if it is well managed, providing revenue that encourages conservation and can also be used to pay for it. But with little previous experience, China's fledgling tourist industry is ill-equipped to cope with the soaring demand projected over the next few years.

Preventing further habitat loss and poaching must be the top priorities for conservation of the giant panda, as for almost every other endangered species. Unfortunately, more is needed. Whatever the precise number of giant pandas now surviving in the wild, those that remain are located in isolated pockets, separated from others of their kind by roads and railways, farmland and clear-felled forest. At present these small populations often number no more than 20 individuals.

Small populations create special problems of conservation. In many animals, social interactions are thought to be an essential preliminary to breeding, helping to synchronise and stimulate reproductive behaviour. It is difficult to be certain if a particular species fails to breed just because there are too few of them for social stimulation to be effective, but this is always a danger. The difficulties encountered in attempting to breed giant pandas in captivity would suggest that for pandas at least, this problem should be taken seriously. Small populations are also in danger because survival is to some extent a matter of chance. From generation to generation the numbers of a species fluctuate around an average figure, the numbers pushed one way and then the other by the vagaries of climate and accidental deaths. A bad year may see a small population wiped out completely, while a chance succession of male or female births may see the sex ratio within the population distorted so badly that the species fails to breed.

A second conservation problem inevitably associated with small populations is the insidious but inevitable loss of genetic variety, a process known to biologists as genetic drift. In a large population genes that are neither particularly beneficial nor particularly damaging are preserved simply because natural selection does not remove them. None the less, the numbers of these genes fluctuate from generation to generation purely by chance. In a population of a thousand, a gene carried by 12 per cent of the animals on average might be represented in 90 animals in one year and 150 the next. In a population of ten, the same fluctuation in frequency means that at the lower level the gene will be lost completely from the gene pool, and can be replaced only by mutation or by the introduction of new animals carrying the gene from outside the population.

A third problem, and perhaps the most dangerous, is that small populations are forced to inbreed. We need look no further than our own species and the history of the European monarchies to see the problems that result from inbreeding. The Hapsburgs, to take just one example, amassed a huge fortune by tactfully marrying the right people at the right time, and then tried hard to hang on to it by marrying each other. Now, the Hapsburgs are best remembered for lending their name to the strangely deformed jaw inherited by the last of their line. The genetic defects and still-births that accompanied their decline are typical of inbred populations, not only of humans but of animals too. Animal breeders have known for many years that mating close relatives leads quickly to disaster.

Given the choice, animals rarely breed with their close relatives. Usually, the young of one sex leave the area in which they were born before they reach maturity, which makes it likely that their partners in their new home will be unrelated. Many animals also recognise their relatives and avoid mating with them even when they do meet. Such 'inbreeding avoidance' has been documented for animals with widely differing social systems and ecological needs—prairie dogs, chimpanzees, horses, jays and woodpeckers are among the best-studied examples. Other animals will mate with relatives only if there are no alternative partners, but breeding often begins later and few litters are raised. Why do animals avoid inbreeding? The evolutionary explanation has to be that it is a waste of reproductive effort, because offspring of close relatives stand little chance of survival (Ralls, 1986).

In order to understand why inbred animals are at risk and what can be done about it, one first needs to know a little about the mechanisms of inheritance. In all mammals every cell (except the egg and sperm, which we shall come back to in a moment) contains two sets of chromosomes, one set inherited from each parent. These contain the DNA, the genetic blueprint that determines exactly what type of proteins the cell manufactures. Each time a cell divides, the DNA it contains is faithfully copied, so that as an animal grows, every single cell in its body contains identical copies of the genetic material inherited from its parents. When producing sperm or eggs, however, a different type of cell division takes place to ensure that only a single copy of the genetic material is passed on to each gamete. When egg and sperm meet and fuse at the moment of fertilisation, the full complement of chromosomes is restored.

Occasionally there are mistakes in copying the DNA, and if this happens during the production of sex cells, the resulting egg or sperm will carry a defective gene. Such alterations are called mutations, and proteins produced from mutated genes are almost always incapable of doing the task of the protein encoded in the original, unchanged gene. Imagine then that a male panda manages to mate, and one of his sperm carrying an altered gene fuses with an egg and begins to develop into an embryo. Often this does not matter much since the developing cub will also be carrying a healthy, working copy of the gene from its mother. Although only one gene is working, the delicate control processes within the cells sense a shortage of the protein and step up production. If the cub breeds successfully, the mutation will spread in the population, but unless close relatives mate with each other no animal is ever likely to be born carrying two copies of the defective gene. In a population in which all the animals are closely related the story is very different. A high percentage carry the same genes, and the chances of a cub inheriting a defective gene from both parents increases accordingly. With no working copy of the gene the young panda is almost certainly doomed to die.

This is not the only way in which inbreeding creates problems. Imagine now that the mutated gene is not totally useless, but that the protein it produces behaves slightly differently. For example, a mutation in the gene coding for the production of haemoglobin might produce a form which binds oxygen more strongly, a change which could help animals living at high altitude. A panda cub carrying genes for both types of haemoglobin might be able to survive over a much wider range of altitudes than pandas with double copies of either the original gene or the mutation. This is a hypothetical example, but a similar situation has been found in white-tailed deer (Chesser et al., 1982). In several populations of white-tailed deer, the older animals are more likely to carry genes for two different types of hae-moglobin than the young. Since it is impossible for the genes to change during an animal's lifetime, the most likely explanation is that animals carrying both genes live longer. Because older stags are more aggressive, they tend to mate more often than young deer, and so they leave more offspring. In biological terms, they are fitter.

Animals carrying different types of the same gene are said to be heterozygous for the gene. The advantages to white-tailed deer of being heterozygous for the haemoglobin gene are unknown, but in the sulphur butterfly, *Colias philodyce*, the mechanism by which being heterozygous can improve an animals survival are better understood. In this case the gene in question produces a protein involved in the breakdown of blood sugars to provide energy for flight. Heterozygotes break down blood sugars faster than homozygotes, enabling them to fly over a wider range and increasing their ability to find food and escape from predators (Watt, 1983).

Inbreeding is dangerous because it exposes harmful mutations and it inevitably produces offspring that carry the same type of each gene. In practice, the results of all this are much the same in a wide variety of different species—reduced life expectancy, low birth-weights, low fertility, small litter size and low reproductive-rate. It is no coincidence that the effects are primarily in areas crucial to reproductive success. Harmful mutations that interfere with these essential functions can only survive in wild populations if the working copy of the gene on the second chromosome can completely take their place. It may not be a matter of life or death if an animal has blue eyes rather than brown, but a gene that interferes with an animal's reproductive ability by definition reduces its evolutionary fitness. Only if such genes remain hidden, their effects dominated by the homologous gene on the other chromosome, can they spread through the population. It is just these 'hidden' genes that inbreeding brings out into the open.

There is already a depressingly long list of species in which inbreeding is suspected to be causing problems for both wild and captive populations. One such species is the golden lion tamarin, a rare and extremely beautiful monkey from Brazil. In 1984 the total wild population of golden lion tamarins was estimated to be less than 400, with perhaps a further 300 animals in captivity (Mallinson, 1984). Many suffer from a genetic defect of the diaphragm which is almost certainly the result of inbreeding. Inbreeding is also responsible for the low birth-weights and high juvenile mortality observed in captive populations of Speke's gazelle. The members of the herd are all descendants from just four animals, and further outbreeding is impossible due to the political unrest in their home range, the border area between Ethiopia and Somalia (Templeton and Read, 1983). High juvenile mortality resulting from inbreeding has now been documented for many species—giraffes, scimitar-horned oryx, black lemurs and mandrills, to name but a few (Ralls and Ballou, 1983).

Inbreeding also results in a second, rather different genetic problem, more insidious since the dangers are not immediately obvious. In a large population where mating is effectively at random, sexual reproduction produces a variety of offspring, some slightly larger or smaller than their parents, or with subtly different spectra of resistance to disease. It is on this variety that natural selection acts, and in each generation only those animals best adapted to their environment reach reproductive age and breed. Small, highly inbred populations that have lost most of their genetic variation may simply not have the necessary resources. This genetic variation may be particularly important in the genes responsible for the generation of antibodies and the operation of the immune system. As Steve O'Brien, a world authority on the genetics of endangered species, puts it: 'Overly inbred populations have a genetic "axe" suspended over them in the form of extreme vulnerability to pathogens in the environment' (O'Brien and Knight, 1987).

The work of this genetic axe can already be seen in another of the animals that O'Brien had studied—the cheetah. About 20,000 cheetahs remain in the wild, but at some point in the past the population apparently crashed to a very few individuals. All cheetahs surviving in the world today are the descendants of this small, relict population. Genetically they are almost identical. Few of their blood-plasma proteins show any genetic variation at all, unlike other African cats which show moderate to high levels of genetic variability. In fact, cheetahs are so genetically similar that skin from one animal grafted onto another is rarely rejected. This operation, usually only possible between identical twins, shows that the immune system of the cheetah does not recognise any of the proteins from another animal's skin as foreign, a genetic homogeneity that makes the cheetah alarmingly susceptible to disease. If a virus manages to infect an animal and multiply without triggering its immune system, it is almost certain to spread right through the population. Once it has fooled one cheetah's immune system, it has fooled them all. In 1982 this point was made graphically by an outbreak of feline infectious peritonitis at the Wildlife Safari Park in Oregon. The virus infected every single cheetah in the park and killed half of them, but no lions (normally quite susceptible to the disease) were infected, and attempts to artificially infect domestic cats for research purposes failed completely (O'Brien et al., 1986).

Inbreeding increases a population's susceptibility to disease and at the same time slows its rate of reproduction. These severe consequences have not yet been seen in wild pandas, although the high infant mortality in zoo-bred pandas could be interpreted as indicating that even in the wild the population is inbred. The limited genetic studies that have been carried out so far do suggest that inbreeding is already resulting in reduced genetic variability. A check on four captive pandas (London Zoo's Chia Chia, Ling Ling and Hsing Hsing from Washington Zoo, and a cub born to the Washington pair) showed only six variations in 300 blood proteins analysed (O'Brien et al., 1984).

The future of the giant panda population in the wild will be secure only if there are enough animals to prevent both the short and long-term effects of inbreeding. But just how many animals is 'enough'? In trying to calculate this figure, the experts are forced to resort to educated guesswork. There is no shortage of species driven to the edge of extinction in the wild that might provide suitable models on which to base a management plan for the panda, but no-one has much experience at dealing with these either. Work with captive populations of vertebrates suggests that if there are more than about 50 randomly interbreeding individuals, natural selection can balance the deterioration of the stock which results from inbreeding. This gives an absolute minimum figure which protects against the short-term effects of inbreeding.

In practice, the minimum population required to achieve even this limited aim will be much larger since, as we saw in Chapter 4, pandas do not interbreed at random. Some males will contribute more genes than others to the next generation because they win more fights at breeding time. Working out the effective population size when breeding is not at random involves some complex theory, but males that do not breed reduce the effective population size dramatically. For example, in a group of 25 females and 25 males of which only 10 males breed, the population is effectively not 50 or even 35 animals, but 28. The evidence also suggests that pandas do not move far from their home range to mate, which strictly limits each animal's choice of partner, although the impact of this is not as serious as might be expected. Add to all this the impact of the low level of genetic variation in the panda population suggested by the O'Brien study mentioned above, and it is reasonable to assume that a population of even 50 animals could be in danger of extinction as a result of inbreeding.

Even more importantly, this minimum figure does not protect the population against the long-term loss of most of its genetic variation. With little genetic variation a species does not have the genetic resources to adapt to a naturally changing environment. To preserve the panda beyond the end of the next century, a larger population is necessary, large enough so that the loss of genetic variation through genetic drift is balanced by the input of new genetic variation through mutation. To calculate the size of this population is even more difficult than to work out the minimum population for short-term survival. The answer depends on the amount of genetic variation already present, the mutation-rate, and the way in which natural selection acts on the population, factors for which there is precious little relevant information. To make even a rough guess we must turn to evidence from fruit flies, whose rapid life-cycle means that a single human researcher can study many successive generations. For fruit flies, gain of variation through mutation and loss through genetic drift act together to maintain typical levels of genetic variance when the population is around 500 (Lande and Barrowclough, 1987). While these are obvious dangers in comparing giant pandas in the wild with fruit flies in the laboratory, the figure is supported by similar studies which predict roughly the same minimum population size for mice.

We do not know enough about conservation genetics to make any more than a rough guess at how serious the situation now is for the panda, but the crude, best-guess estimate is alarming. The smallest viable population for short-term survival is 50 randomly interbreeding animals. Nine of the panda reserves were estimated to contain less than 50 pandas in 1980. The smallest viable population for long-term survival is 500 randomly interbreeding individuals. The remaining three panda reserves each contain less than 150 animals, and in at least one reserve these are subdivided into two subpopulations which are separated by agricultural land and cannot inter-breed. In all, it is estimated that the giant pandas now exist in about 35 isolated populations and that most of these contain fewer than 20 individuals. Taken in isolation the much publicised figure of 1,000 pandas surviving in the wild sounds reassuring, but these calculations seem to show that the giant panda is already in serious trouble.

Fortunately, things may not be quite as bad as they seem. We have already seen that small and isolated populations tend to lose genetic variation through the process of genetic drift, but this is a random process. Some populations lose genes which may be retained in other groups, and vice versa. The general effect of dividing a population into small isolated groups is that although the genetic variation within each subpopulation disappears more rapidly, the variation in the population as a whole disappears rather more slowly. As already noted above, inbreeding in these small isolated populations still tends to reduce the numbers of animals carrying different copies of the same gene, but computer simulations show that this can be largely corrected by occasional migrations of animals between the subpopulations (Boecklen, 1986).

The totally wild panda living in blissful isolation and free from all human interference has probably gone for ever. With it goes a small part of what is most beautiful about our planet—the mystery of how life with its intricate and delicate webs of interaction sustains itself. To prevent more from being lost, we must interfere. Interference now requires more than the prevention of slaughter by the greedy, and the control of destruction by farmers hungry for land and timber. Now we must also take control of the panda's genetic future, monitoring each population and carefully manipulating them to ensure that the species survives.

The least invasive and manipulative method for doing this is that proposed in the management plan for the giant panda worked out by the World Wildlife Fund, which stresses the importance of establishing 'corridors' between isolated populations of pandas to encourage migration between them, and improving the protection of the panda habitat outside the reserves. Theory predicts that the rate of migration along these corridors need not be substantial—less than 1 per cent of the animals need to move between populations in each generation to balance the loss of genetic variation through genetic drift. Since there are serious doubts about the accuracy of the predictions from the infant science of conservation genetics, this might just possibly be all that is required. Only through a long-term programme which carefully monitors the genetic health of a substantial proportion of the panda population will we find out. Sadly, it is just this type of expensive, long-term project that least appeals to those who might fund it. But without this type of genetic monitoring, it will be impossible to judge the long-term prospects for the panda, or to know whether or not more intensive management is necessary.

One management strategy that might be appropriate if the planned corridors do not promote sufficient migration and mixing of gene pools, is to capture pandas in one area and release them in another. Being vegetarians surrounded by food, pandas might be expected to adapt quite easily to being moved around in this way, even though they do not normally move far outside a fairly well-defined home range. Previous experience of the capture and release of giant pandas is hardly encouraging, however. According to the official Chinese Xinhua News Agency, 14 pandas had been returned to the wild by May 1986 following the panda rescue programme in which animals were taken into captivity after the flowering and death of the bamboo in the late 1970s and early 1980s. Unfortunately, as far as is known, only three of these carried radio collars. One died soon after release of unknown causes. From the radio signal the body appeared to be halfway down a precipitous cliff. The other two animals returned to take up residence close to their original ranges. There is consequently no good evidence that pandas are able to adjust to relocation. Capture and release might be possible as a means of restocking areas in which populations have previously reached low levels or died out. However, more work needs to be done before animals can be introduced into areas where they must compete for resources with the indigenous population, if there is to be any guarantee that the introduced animals will survive, let alone breed successfully. If this fails, one final possibility is to capture animals in the wild, and either artificially inseminate them with sperm from 'foreign' males or transfer embryos from captive females. However, while this approach is fine in theory, in practice the present level of expertise in captive breeding is woefully inadequate, and there is little hope that it will be practical to use such management techniques with pandas in the near future.

Little information is as yet available on potential genetic problems among wild populations of the red panda, although all the evidence suggests that like the giant panda, red pandas are increasingly confined to small and isolated populations. It is already clear from studies of the zoo population that red pandas are naturally outbreeding animals. Inbreeding in the zoo population has shown that the young of closely related animals are less likely to survive than the offspring of matings between unrelated animals, and also that females mated to relatives are less likely to survive themselves to raise another litter (Roberts, 1982c).

Poaching, forest clearance, expanding agriculture, tourism and genetic deterioration—for anyone with even a passing interest in conservation this list will be painfully familiar since these dangers threaten so many rare species. Time will only increase the pressures. To save the giant panda in the wild is going to be a formidable task, requiring an extension of the existing reserve system, the movement of more people from sensitive areas, the replanting of trees and bamboo to create corridors between isolated patches of habitat, the education of the local people, the setting up of an effective system of forest guards to stamp out poaching and woodcutting, further research on panda genetics and captive breeding, and not a little good luck.

Even ignoring the difficulties that might be posed by inbreeding, the relatively simple operation of managing the animals themselves may hold unforeseen difficulties. Most predators in the reserves have now been eliminated, and there is already evidence that where hunting has been successfully controlled, takin numbers have increased rapidly. Takin probably also benefit from the increased growth of secondary vegetation which occurs following timber-cutting. Although detailed studies have not been done, there is a fear that the large number of takin may already be destabilising the delicately balanced ecosystem. Takin spend the summers in the high alpine meadows feeding on grass and other tender mountain vegetation, often descending to the valleys in winter to eat the buds and bark of deciduous trees. Takin also eat bamboo, albeit in small quantities. They are consequently in direct competition with pandas for food, although bamboo is only a minor component of the takin's diet and it is unlikely that this is really a significant problem. Nevertheless, with their chief predators the wild dogs and leopards already hunted to extinction in some areas and rare throughout these mountains, the conservation of takin will be a delicate balancing act (Schaller *et al.*, 1986).

Conserving the pandas is going to cost millions of pounds. If we are not serious about succeeding we might as well give up now, recover the costs of the operation so far by hunting down the last remaining animals to sell off as door-mats, and forget the whole business.

The position of Western governments in the past has been that conservation projects in foreign lands are a matter for individuals, and are best supported through donations to charitable organisations. The recent announcement by the British government that it is to begin donating money to the World Wildlife Fund to help with conservation of rainforests may signal a long-overdue change. However, the task of saving the giant panda in the wild may be beyond the means of a single charitable organisation. Nor is it necessarily desirable that the collection and distribution of funds should be in the hands of a single agency. The World Wildlife Fund must constantly walk a tightrope, persuading the public that its goals are achievable, and that its strategies are working. Blunders cannot be admitted, for fear that the people who trustingly hand over their money in the hope of doing something for the world's threatened species will lose confidence. In the long term this must damage not only the World Wildlife Fund, but the prospects for success in their objectives. By delegating responsibility to other organisations the Fund could easily avoid these problems, and in so doing the project to save the panda and its natural habitat might also gain more political and financial muscle. Increasingly, conservation requires more than detailed academic research and cosy agreement on the delineation of park boundaries and the management of tourism. It also needs anti-poaching units and effective policing to prevent illegal timber-cutting—activities that are certain to cause conflict between conservation agencies and most governments.

To raise more cash and to create a structure that overcomes these inherent conflicts, new alliances must be forged. It is not only agencies involved in wildlife conservation that might have a role to play. Conservation of the forests on the steep mountain slopes is as important to the long-term security of the almost 100 million people living on the Sichuan plain as it is to the pandas.

If we manage to avoid a nuclear holocaust and succeed in ensuring the survival of our own species, it is likely that present generations will be judged by those that come after us on the extent to which we limit the damage caused by the holocaust we are inflicting on the creatures with which we share this planet. As custodians of the symbol of conservation, the Chinese are in this respect in an unenviable position. In the words of William Conway, director of the New York Zoological Society, 'There are probably fewer pandas extant than there are Rembrandts. We ought to give them as much reverence as we give the works of man.' The comparison is aptly chosen, for the loss of a Rembrandt would be final and would diminish our culture. How much poorer we would be without the entire body of his work—although of course we could always look at reproductions. A print carries something of the power of a great work of art, but a photograph—even a film—can capture no more than a moment in the life of an animal.

As early as 1934 one of the first Western travellers through western Sichuan, Herbert Stevens, wrote:

> Protected as this rare 'survival' is by the characteristic features of this habitat which for distorted and inaccessible terrain can seldom be equalled, nevertheless a census of its numbers is desirable, but of far greater import is the need for a Sanctuary . . . If this plea should act as a stimulus to those with like sympathies before it is too late to save *Ailuropoda melanoleuca* from extinction it will have served its purpose, should it be ever so pious a hope with only the remotest chance of materialization. (Stevens, 1934)

The panda is not yet safe from extinction, but a change in attitude has already made possible the first step along the path to security—the establishment of the panda reserves. A truly certain future for the panda will require a change in public awareness of a magnitude as great as that which made Stevens's 'pious hope' a reality, but the path has been marked out and it is now simply a matter of deciding whether or not we want to make the journey. As George Schaller points out in the preface to his authoritative book (Schaller, 1985), 'There are two giant pandas, the one that exists in our mind, and the one that lives in its wilderness home.' The chances are that unless the popular enthusiasm for the giant panda can be translated into effective conservation measures, both giant and red pandas will become extinct together, and we will be left only with the animal of our imaginations.

Note

1. As poaching continues, sentencing is becoming tougher, and in October 1989 the first executions for trading in skins were carried out.

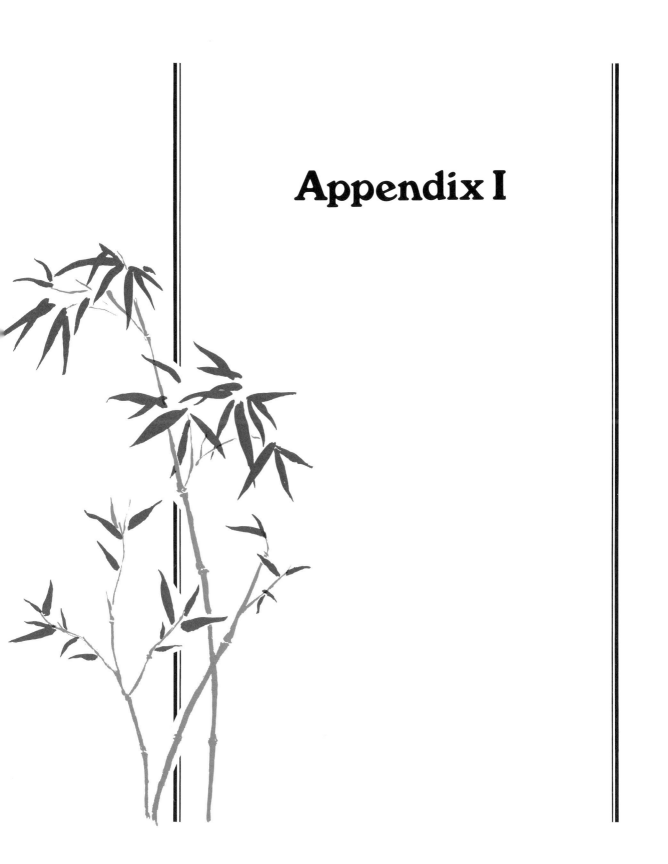

Appendix I

Bamboo synonyms

Because bamboo flowers rarely, and because the natural habitat of those species important as food for pandas has long been inaccessible, the scientific naming of bamboo species is in disarray. In some cases, each writer who has studied a species has given it a different name. In this book I have followed the system adopted by Yi Tongpei, who has studied the bamboos from giant panda habitat for more than 20 years and has collected and examined all the relevant species. I am not qualified to enter the debate on the merits and status of the alternative names, and the adoption of this system does not imply disagreement with other authors. The table below is provided to help anyone who is interested in studying this difficult and confusing area further.

Schaller[1]	Campbell[2]	Yi Tongpei[3]
Sinarundinaria fangiana	*Arundinaria fangiana*	*Gelidocalamus fangianus*
Sinarundinaria ferax	*Sinarundinaria ferax*	*Fargesia ferax*
Sinarundinaria chungii	*Yushania chungii*	*Yushania chungii*
Fargesia spathacea	*Fargesia robusta*	*Fargesia robusta*
		Fargesia aurita (Qin Ling)
Sinarundinaria nitida	*Sinarundinaria nitida*	*Fargesia nitida* (agreed by Schaller)
Fargesia scabrida	*Sinarundinaria scabrida*	*Fargesia scabrida*
Fargesia denudata	*Fargesia denudata*	*Fargesia denudata*

Notes

1. *Giant Pandas of Wolong.*
2. J.J.N. Campbell (1988) *Sino-Himalayan Bamboos: Towards a Synthesis of Western and Eastern Knowledge*, paper presented at the International Bamboo Conference, Prafrance, 7–9 June.
3. Yi Tongpei (1985) Classification and distribution of the food bamboos of the giant panda (I) *Journal of Bamboo Research 4 (2)*.
   Yi Tongpei (1985) The classification and distribution of bamboos naturally eaten by the giant panda. *Abstracts International Bamboo Conference, Mayaqüez, Puerto Rico 1985.* American Bamboo Society: 5–6.

Appendix II

Bamboos known to be eaten by pandas in their native habitat

Min Mountains

Major food sources
Fargesia nitida
F. denudata
F. scabrida
F. rufa
F. robusta
F. aurita
Bashania fargesii
Gelidocalamus fangianus
Yushania chungii
Secondary food sources
Phyllostachys rigita
P. nidularia
P. nigra
F. angustissima
Neosinocalamus saxatilis
N. affinis

Qionglai Mountains

G. fangianus
Y. chungii
F. ferax
F. emaculata
P. nidularia
F. angustissima
F. canaliculata
Chimnobambusa pachystachys

Qinling Mountains

F. aurita
Y. chungii

Daxiang and Xiaoxiang Mountains

C. szechuanensis
G. fangianus
Y. chungii
F. jiulongensis
F. pauciflora
F. adpressa
Y. lineolata

Liang Mountains

Qiongzhuea tumidinoda
Q. macrophylla
Q. rigidula
Q. opienensis
G. fangianus
Y. chungii
F. pauciflora
Indocalamus longiauritus

Appendix III

Giant pandas taken out of China to foreign zoos

Name	Sex	Zoo	Arrival	Death
Su Lin	M	Brookfield Chicago USA	Feb. 1937	April 1937
Diana/Mei Mei	M	Brookfield Chicago USA	Feb. 1938	August 1942
Jennie	F	London Zoo*	—	1937
Pandora	F	Bronx New York USA	June 1938	May 1941
Baby/Ming	F	London Zoo UK	Dec. 1938	Dec. 1944
Grumpy/Tang	M	London Zoo UK	Dec. 1938	April 1940
Dopey/Sung	M	London Zoo UK	Dec. 1938	Dec. 1939
Happy	M	London/St Louis USA	June 1939	March 1946
Grandma	F	London UK	Dec. 1938	Jan. 1939
Mei Lan	M	Brookfield Chicago USA	Nov. 1939	Sept. 1953
Pan	M	Bronx New York USA	May 1939	May 1940
Pao Pei	F	New York/St Louis USA	Sept. 1939	June 1952
Pan Dee	F	Bronx New York USA	Dec. 1941	Oct. 1945
Pan Dah	M?	Bronx New York USA	Dec. 1941	Oct. 1951
Lien Ho	M	London Zoo UK	May 1946	Feb. 1950
Unnamed	?	Bronx New York USA**	—	1946
Ping Ping	M	Moscow Zoo USSR	May 1957	May 1961
Chi Chi	F	London Zoo UK	Sept. 1958	July 1972
An An	M	Moscow Zoo USSR	Aug. 1959	Oct. 1972
Unnamed	?	Pyongyang North Korea	June 1965	Unknown
Unnamed	?	Pyongyang North Korea	June 1965	Unknown
San Xing	F	Pyongyang North Korea	Oct. 1971	Unknown
Lin Lin	M	Pyongyang North Korea	Oct. 1971	Unknown
Lan Lan	F	Ueno Zoo Tokyo Japan	Oct. 1972	Sept. 1979
Ling Ling	F	National Zoo Washington USA	April 1972	Living
Kang Kang	M	Ueno Zoo Tokyo Japan	Oct. 1972	June 1980
Hsing Hsing	M	National Zoo Washington USA	April 1972	Living

Ching Ching	F	London Zoo UK	Sept. 1974	July 1975
Chia Chia	M	London Zoo UK/ Chapultepec Zoo Mexico	Sept. 1974	Living
Li Li	M	Paris Zoo France	Dec. 1973	April 1974
Huan Huan	F	Ueno Zoo Tokyo Japan	Jan. 1980	Living
Yen Yen	M	Paris Zoo France	Dec. 1973	Living
Chang Chang	M	Madrid Zoo Spain	Dec. 1978	Living
Ying Ying	F	Chapultepec Zoo Mexico	Sept. 1975	Jan. 1989
Pe Pe	M	Chapultepec Zoo Mexico	Sept. 1975	Dec. 1988
Shao Shao	F	Madrid Zoo Spain	Dec. 1978	Oct. 1983
Fei Fei	M	Ueno Zoo Tokyo Japan	Nov. 1982	Living
Bao Bao	M	Berlin Zoo West Germany	Nov. 1980	Living
Tian Tian	F	Berlin Zoo West Germany	Nov. 1980	Feb. 1984
Dan Dan	M	Pyongyang North Korea	March 1979	Unknown

*Died at sea before reaching England.
**Died before reaching New York.

Bibliography

ANON. (1934) *China Journal 21(4)*:170

ANON. (1937a) Mrs Harkness comes and goes. *China Journal 27*:145

ANON. (1937b) The giant panda's diet. *China Journal 27*:209–30

ANON. (1938a) Ruth Harkness completes west China expedition. *China Journal 28*:37–8

ANON. (1938b) Baby giant panda exhibited in Shanghai. *China Journal 28*:97

ANON. (1938c) The latest panda news. *China Journal 29(1)*:60

ANON. (1945) The death of one giant panda. *Animal Kingdom 48(6)*:188

ANON. (1946) A giant panda is promised. *Animal Kingdom 49(6)*:217

ANON. (1966) Animals news. *Animals 8(12)*:329

ANON. (1979) The Japanese weep for Lan Lan. *Newsweek (International edition)* 17 September: 23

ANON. (1988) The panda—edging towards extinction. *Animals International 8(27)*:10

BERTRAM, B.C.R. AND GORE, M.A. (1985) Notes on the giant panda studbook. *Bongo Sonderband 10*:13–20

BHATT, D.D. (1977) *Natural History and Economic Botany of Nepal.* Orient Longman, New Delhi

BLEIJENBERG, M.C.K. (1984) When is a carnivore not a carnivore? When it's a panda. In A.R. Glatston (ed.) *The Red Panda or Lesser Panda Studbook No. 3.* The Royal Rotterdam Zoological and Botanical Gardens, Rotterdam, The Netherlands: 23–36

BLOWER, J. (1985) Conservation priorities in Burma. *Oryx 19(2)*:79–85

BOECKLEN, W.J. (1986) Optimal design of nature reserves: consequences of genetic drift. *Biological Conservation 38(4)*:323–38

BONNEY, R.C., WOOD, D.J. AND KLEIMAN, D.G. (1982) Endocrine correlates of behavioural oestrus in the female giant panda (*Ailuropoda melanoleuca*) and associated hormonal changes in the male. *Journal of Reproduction and Fertility 64(1)*:209–15H

BRAMBELL, M.R. (1974) London Zoo's giant panda (*Ailuropoda melanoleuca*) Chi Chi, 1957–1972. *International Zoo Yearbook 14*: 163–4

BRETSCHNEIDER, E. (1898) *The History of European Botanical Discoveries in China.* St Petersburg 1898, reprinted 1962 by Zentral-Antiquariat, Leipzig

BÜCHNER, E. (1892) Die Säugethiere der Ganssu-Expedition (1884–87). *Bulletin de l'Académie impériale des sciences de St Petersbourg N.S. 2 34*:97–118

BURGMAN, M.A., AKCAKAYA, H.R. AND LOEW, S.S. (1988) The use of extinction models for species conservation. *Biological Conservation 43(1)*: 9–25

BUSH, M. AND ROBERTS, M.S. (1977) Distemper in captive red pandas (*Ailurus fulgens*). *International Zoo Yearbook 17*: 194–6

CAMPBELL, J.J.N. (1987) The history of Sino-Himalayan bamboo flowering, droughts and sunspots. *Journal of Bamboo Research 6(1)*: 2–15

—— AND QIN, Z.S. (1983) Interaction of giant pandas, bamboos and people. *Journal of the American Bamboo Society 4(1&2)*:1–35

CARTER, T.D. (1937) The giant panda. *Animal Kingdom 40(1)*: 6–14

CATTON, C. (1987) Hua Hua eschews cuddly reputation. *BBC Wildlife 5(12)*:641

CHAUDHURI, M., KLEIMAN, D.G., WILDT, D.E., BUSH, M., FRANK, E.S. AND THAU, R.B. (1988) Urinary steroid concentrations during natural and gonadotrophin-induced estrus and pregnancy in the giant panda *Ailuropoda melanoleuca*. *Journal of Reproduction and Fertility 84(1)*:23–8

CHESSER, R.K., SMITH, M.H., JOHNS, P.E., MANLOVE, M.N., STRANEY, D.O. AND BACCUS, R. (1982) Spatial, temporal and age-dependent heterozygosity of beta-hemoglobin in white-tailed deer. *Journal of Wildlife Management 46*: 983–90

CHIN, H. (1979) China's first baby giant panda reproduced by artificial insemination. *International Zoo News No. 157 26(1)*:8–10

CIOCHON, R.L. (1988) Paleoanthropological research in the pleistocene karst caves of northern Vietnam. *American Journal of Physical Anthropology 75(2)*:196

CLARKE, G. (1987) The whole world goes pandas; two Chinese ambassadors receive cheers in Bronx Zoo. *Time May 11*:52 (European edition)

COHN, J.P. (1988) Captive breeding for conservation. *Bioscience 38(5)*:312–16

CONOVER, G.K. AND GITTLEMAN, J.L. (1989) Scent-marking in captive red pandas (*Ailurus fulgens*). *Zoo Biology 8*: (in press)

CUVIER, F. (1824–42) *Histoire naturelle des mammifères, avec des figures originales, colorées, desinées d'apres des animaux vivants. (Paris) 2*:1–3

DAVID, A. (1871) Rapport adressé a M.M. Les Professeurs–administrateurs du muséum d'histoire naturelle. *Nouvelle Archives du muséum d'histoire naturelle Paris 7*:75–100

—— (1874) Journal d'un voyage dans le centre de la Chine. *Nouvelle Archives du muséum d'histoire naturelle Paris (Bulletin) 10*:1–95

—— (1875) *Journal de mon troisième voyage d'exploration dans l'empire Chinoise 2*: Librairie Hachette et Cie

DAVIS, D.D. (1964) The giant panda: a morphological study of evolutionary mechanisms. *Fieldiana (Chicago Museum of Natural History) Memoirs (Zoology) 3*:1–339

DE HAVILLAND, M. (1987) *The Fabulous Panda*. Pan Books, London:21

(1987) *The Times* Friday 13 March

DEMMER, H. (1958a) The first giant panda since the war has reached the western world. *International Zoo News 5(4)*:99–101

—— (1958b) Chi Chi's new home at the London Zoo. *International Zoo News 5(6)*:171–2

DERBY, O.A. (1879) Rats in Brazil and their connection with the flowering of bamboo. *Indian Forestry 5*:177–8

DE WULF, R., MACKINNON, J.R. AND CAI, W.S. (1988) Remote sensing for wildlife management: Giant panda habitat mapping from LANDSAT MSS images. *Geocarto International 1988(1)*:41–50

DOMICO, T. (1988) *Bears of the World*. Facts on File, New York and Oxford:48

EISENBERG, J.F. AND KLEIMAN, D.G. (1977) The usefulness of behaviour studies in developing captive breeding programmes for mammals. *International Zoo Yearbook 17*:81–9

FENG, Z., ZHENG, C. AND CAI, Q. (1981) On mammals from southeastern Xizang. In D.S. Liu, (ed.) *Geological and Ecological Studies of Qinghai-Xizang Plateau 2*. Science Press, Beijing and Gordon and Breade, New York: 1013–16

FLEMING, W.B. (1987) A look at the little known red panda. *Nepal Traveller 4(1)*:10–12

—— (1988) The elusive red panda. *Nepal Traveller 5(6)*:21–23

FLOWER, W.H. AND LYDEKKER, R. (1891) *Mammals Living and Extinct.* Adam and Charles Black, London

FOCKELMANN, O. (1964) Unpublished letter to Richard J. Reynolds III

—— (1985) A panda shipment in 1938. *Bongo Sonderband 10*:7–12

FOX, H.M. (1949) *Abbé David's Diary.* Harvard University Press, Cambridge, Mass.: xvi

GENTZ, E.J. (1987) Genic divergence between *Ailurus fulgens fulgens* and *Ailurus fulgens styani.* In A.R. Glatston (ed.) *The Red Panda Conference.* The Royal Rotterdam Zoological and Botanical Gardens (in press)

GERVAIS, P. (1875) De l'*Ursus melanoleucus* de l'Abbé Armand David. *Gervais Journal of Zoology 4*:79–87

GIANT PANDA EXPEDITION (1974) A survey of the giant panda (*Ailuropoda melanoleuca*) in the Wanglang Natural Reserve, Pingwu, northern Sichuan, China. *Acta Zoologica Sinica 20(2)*:162–73 (in Chinese)

GINSBURG, L., INGVAT, R. AND SEN, S. (1982) A middle pleistocene Loangian cave fauna in northern Thailand. *Comptes Rendus des Séances de l'Académie des Sciences, Série III, Sciences de la Vie 294(4)*:189–92

GITTLEMAN, J.L. (1987) Lactation energetics and a general model for protracted growth in the red panda (*Ailurus fulgens*). *The Red Panda Conference*, The Royal Rotterdam Botanical and Zoological Gardens (in press)

—— (1988) Behavioural energetics of lactation in a herbivorous carnivore, the red panda (*Ailurus fulgens*). *Ethology 79(1)*:13–24

GLATSTON, A.R. (1980) *Introduction.* In A.R. Glatston (ed.) *The Red or Lesser Panda Studbook No. 1 (1978–9).* Stichting Koninklijke Rotterdamse Diergaard: 3–10

—— AND ROBERTS, M.S. (1988) The current status and future prospects of the red panda (*Ailurus fulgens*) studbook population. *Zoo Biology 7*:47–59

GOLDMAN, D., GIRI, P.R. AND O'BRIEN, S.J. (1989) Molecular genetic-distance estimates among the Ursidae as indicated by one- and two-dimensional protein electrophoresis. *Evolution 32(12)*:282–95

GREEN, M. (1986) The creature with the golden gland. *BBC Wildlife 4(7)*:327–30

HAMILTON, W.J. AND HEPPNER, F. (1967) Radiant solar energy and the function of black homeotherm pigmentation: an hypothesis. *Science 155*:196–7

HARKNESS, R. (1938) *The Lady and the Panda.* Nicholson and Watson, London

HEUVELMANS, B. (1966) Unpublished letter to Richard J. Reynolds III

HODGSON, B.H. (1847) On the cat-toed subplantigrades of the sub-Himalayas. *Journal of the Asiatic Society of Bengal 16*:1113–29

HRDY, S.B. (1974) Male–male competition and infanticide among the langurs (*Presbytis entellus*) of Abu, Rajasthan. *Folia primatologica 22(1)*:19–58

HU, J. (1985) Ecographic distribution of the great panda. In T. Kawamichi (ed.) *Contemporary Mammalogy in China and Japan.* (Mammalogical Society of Japan)

HUDSON, G.J., BAILEY, P.A., JOHN, P.M.V., MONSALVE, L., GARCIA DEL CAMPO, A-L., TAYLOR, D.C. AND KAY, J.D.S. (1984) Composition of milk from *Ailuropoda melanoleuca*, the giant panda. *Veterinary Record 115(10)*:252

IUCN CONSERVATION MONITORING CENTRE (1988) *IUCN Red List of Threatened Animals.* International Union for Conservation of Nature and Natural Resources, Gland, Switzerland and Cambridge, UK

JANZEN, D.H. (1976) Why bamboos wait so long to flower. *Annual Review of Ecology and Systematics 7*:347–91

JOHNSON, K.G., SCHALLER, G.B. AND HU, J. (1988) Comparative behavior of red and giant pandas in the Wolong reserve, China. *Journal of Mammalogy 69(3)*:552–64

KAWAMURA, S. (1927) On the periodical flowering of the bamboo. *Japanese Journal of Botany 3*:335–49

KELLER, R. (1980) The social behaviour of captive lesser pandas (*Ailurus fulgens*) with some management suggestions. In A.R. Glatston (ed.) *The Red or Lesser Panda Studbook No. 1 (1978–9)*. Stichting Koningklijke Rotterdamse Diergaard: 39–55

KILBORN, L.G. (1965) Unpublished letter to Richard J. Reynolds III

KLEIMAN, D.G. (1983) Ethology and reproduction of captive giant pandas. *Zeitschrift Für Tierpsychologie 62(1)*:1–46

—— KARESH, W.B. AND CHU, P.R. (1979) Behavioural changes associated with oestrus in the giant panda (*Ailuropoda melanoleuca*) with comments on female proceptive behaviour. *International Zoo Yearbook 19*:217–23

LANDE, R. AND BARROWCLOUGH, G.F. (1987) Effective population size, genetic variation and their use in population management. In M.E. Soulé (ed.) *Viable populations for conservation*. Cambridge University Press, Cambridge: 87–124

LANG, E.M. (1977) What are endangered species? *International Zoo Yearbook 17*:2–14

LANKESTER, E.R. (1901) On the affinities of *Ailuropus melanoleucus*, A. Milne-Edwards. *Transactions of the Linnean Society Second Series Zoology 8*:163–5

LEONE, C.A. AND WIENS, A.L. (1956) Comparative serology of carnivores. *Journal of Mammalogy 37(1)*:11–23

LIU, W-X. (1988) Litter size and survival rate in captive giant pandas (*Ailuropoda melanoleuca*). *International Zoo Yearbook 27*:304–7

LIU, J. (1984) On the morphological features of the intestine and mesentery of the giant panda (*Ailuropoda melanoleuca*). *Acta Zoologica Sinica 30(4)*:317–23

LOSEBY, R. (1938) Five Giant Pandas. *The Field 172*:1532

LYSTER, R.L.J. (1976) Mammary gland secretion. *Transactions of the Zoological Society of London 33*:141–5

MA, G-Y. (1985) Preliminary observations on the growth of bamboo in the valley Baishuijiang. *Chinese Journal of Zoolgy 20(3)*:34–8 (in Chinese)

MACHLIS, G. AND JOHNSON, K. (1987) Panda outposts. *National Parks 61*:14–16

MACKINNON, J.R. AND QIU, M.J. (1986) A management strategy to save the giant panda and its habitat. Preliminary draft (unpublished), World Wide Fund for Nature (WWF), Gland

MALLINSON, J. (1984) Lion tamarin survival hangs in balance. *Oryx 18*:72–8

MATTHIESEN, P. (1978) *The Snow Leopard*. Reprinted by kind permission of Viking Penguin Inc., New York, a division of Penguin USA Inc. (1978) and Chatto and Windus, London, (1980):33

MAYR, E. (1986) Uncertainty in science: is the giant panda a bear or a racoon? *Nature 323*:769–71

MACNAB, B.K. (1988) Energy conservation in a tree kangaroo *Dendrolagus-matschiei* and the red panda *Ailurus fulgens*. *Physiological Zoology 61(3)*:280–92

MILNE-EDWARDS, A. (1869) Extrait d'une lettre de même datée de la principauté Thibétaine (indépendante) de Mou-pin, le 21 mars 1869. *Nouvelle Archives du Muséum d'Histoire Naturelle. Paris (Bulletin) 5:*11–13

——— (1870) Note sur quelques mammifères du Thibet oriental. *Comptes Rendu hebdominaires des Séances de l'Académie des Sciences 70:*341–2

MILTON, K. (1978) Behavioural adaptations to leaf-eating by the mantled howler monkey (*Alouatta palliata*). In G.G. Montgomery (ed.) *The Ecology of Arboreal Folivores.* Smithsonian Institution Press: 525–50

MIVART, S. (1885) On the anatomy, classification, and distribution of the Arctoidea. *Proceedings of the Zoological Society of London*: 340–404

MOORE, H.D.M., BUSH, M., CELMA, M., GARCIA, A-L., HARTMAN, T.D., HEARNE, J.P., HODGES, J.K., JONES, D.M., KNIGHT, J.A., MONSALVE, L. AND WILDT, D.E. (1984) Artificial insemination in the giant panda (*Ailuropoda melanoleuca*). *Journal of Zoology London 203(2):*269–78

MORRIS, R. AND MORRIS, D. (1966) *Men and Pandas.* McGraw-Hill, New York

MURATA, K., MASAYUKI, T. AND MURAKAMI, N. (1986) The relationship between the pattern of urinary oestrogen and behavioural changes in the giant panda *Ailuropoda melanoleuca. International Zoo Yearbook 24/25:*274–9

NAKAZATO, R., SAGAWA, Y., TAJIMA, H., KASAI, N., YAMANOBE, M., TASHIRO, K. AND ASAKURA, S. (1985) Giant pandas at Ueno Zoo. *Bongo Sonderband 10:*33–42

O'BRIEN, S.J., GOLDMAN, D., KNIGHT, J., MOORE, H.D., WILDT, D.E., BUSH, M., MONTALI, R.J. AND KLEIMAN, D. (1984) Giant panda paternity. *Science 223:*1127–9

———, NASH, W.G., WILDT, D.E., BUSH, M.E. AND BENVENISTE, R.E. (1985) A molecular solution to the riddle of the giant panda's phylogeny. *Nature 317:*140–4

———, WILDT, D.E. AND BUSH, M. (1986) The cheetah in genetic peril. *Scientific American 254(5):*68–76

———, AND KNIGHT, J.A. (1987) The future of the giant panda. *Nature 325:*758–9

OFTEDAL, O.T. AND GITTLEMAN, J.L. (1989) Patterns of energy output during reproduction in carnivores. In J.L. Gittleman (ed.) *Carnivore Behaviour, Ecology and Evolution.* Chapman and Hall, London: 355–78

PEKING ZOO (1974) Observation on the propagation of giant panda and development of the young panda. *Acta Zoologica Sinica 20(2):*139–47 (in Chinese)

PEN, H.S. (1943) Some notes on the giant panda. *Bulletin of the Fan Memorial Institute of Biology, Peiping* N.S.: 1(1) 64–70

PRICE, M.R. (1986) The reintroduction of the Arabian oryx (*Oryx leucoryx*) into Oman. *International Zoo Yearbook 24/25:*179–88

PRINCÉE, F.P.G. (1988) Genetic variation in the zoo population of the red panda subspecies *Ailurus fulgens fulgens. Zoo Biology 7:*219–31

RALLS, K., AND BALLOU, J. (1983) Extinction: Lessons from zoos. In C.M. Schonewald-Cox, S.M. Chambers, B. MacBride and L. Thomas (eds) *Genetics and Conservation*: 164–84

———, HARVEY, P.H. AND LYLES, A.M. (1986) Inbreeding in natural populations of birds and mammals. In Soulé, M.E. (ed.) *Conservation Biology: The Science of Scarcity and Diversity.* Sinauer Associates Inc. Massachusetts: 35–56

REID, D.G., HU, J., DONG, C., WANG, W. AND HUANG, Y. (1989) Giant panda *Ailuropoda melanolceuca* behaviour and carrying capacity following a bamboo die-off. *Biological Conservation 49*: in press

ROBERTS, M.S. (1982a) On the subspecies of the red panda *Ailurus fulgens*. In A.R. Glatston (ed.) *The Red or Lesser Panda Studbook No. 2*. The Royal Rotterdam Zoological and Botanical Gardens, Rotterdam, The Netherlands: 13–24

—— (1982b) The fire fox. *Animal Kingdom 85(1)*:20–7

—— (1982c) Demographic trends in a captive population of red pandas (*Ailurus fulgens*). *Zoo Biology 1*:119–26

—— Report on the red panda. *The Red or Lesser Panda Studbook No. 4*. In A. R. Glatston (ed.) The Royal Rotterdam Zoological and Botanical Gardens, Rotterdam, The Netherlands: 39–46

—— AND KESSLER, D.S. (1979) Reproduction in red pandas, *Ailurus fulgens* (Carnivora: Ailuropodidae). *Journal of Zoology London 188(2)*:235–49

—— AND GITTLEMAN, J.L. (1984) *Ailurus fulgens. Mammalian species 222*:1–8

ROOSEVELT, T. AND ROOSEVELT, K. (1929) *Trailing the Giant Panda*. Reprinted by kind permission of Charles Scribner's Sons, an imprint of Macmillan Publishing Company. Copyright 1929 Charles Scribner's Sons; copyright renewed 1957 Eleanor B. Roosevelt and Belle Wyatt Roosevelt

RUSSELL, G.M. (1965) Unpublished letter to R. Reynolds

SAGE, D. (1935) In quest of the giant panda. *Natural History 35*:309–20

SARGENT, C. (1985) The forests of Bhutan. *Ambio 14(2)*:75–80

SARICH, V. (1973) The giant panda is a bear. *Nature 245*:218–20

SCHALLER, G.B. (1963) *The Serengeti Lion: a Study of Predator–Prey Relations*. Chicago, University of Chicago Press

—— (1986) Secrets of the giant panda. *National Geographic 169(3)*:284–309

—— (1987) Bamboo shortage not the only cause of panda decline. *Nature 327*:562

—— (1988) The giant panda. *World Magazine 15*:22–8

——, HU, J., PAN, W. AND ZHU, J. (1985) *The Giant Pandas of Wolong*. University of Chicago Press, Chicago

——, TENG, Q., PAN, W., QIN, Z., WANG, X., HU, J. AND SHEN, H. (1986) Feeding behaviour of Sichuan takin (*Budorcas taxicolor*). *Mammalia 50(3)*:311–22

——, TENG, Q., JOHNSON, K.G., WANG, X., SHEN, H. AND HA, J. (1989) The feeding ecology of giant pandas and Asiatic black bears in the Tangjiahe Reserve, China. In J.L. Gittleman (ed.) *Carnivore Behaviour, Ecology and Evolution*. Chapman and Hall, London: 212–41

SCHELL, O. (1985) *To Get Rich is Glorious: China in the 80's*. Reprinted by kind permission of Pantheon books, a Division of Random House, Inc. and Quartet Books Ltd.

SHELDON, W.G. (1937) Notes on the giant panda. *Journal of Mammalogy 18*:13–19

SHEN, S., ABLES, E.D. AND XIAO, Q-Z. (1982) The Chinese view of wildlife. *Oryx 26(4)*:340–7

SITWELL, N. (1977) The inscrutable panda and Professor Hu. *International Wildlife 7*:36

SMITH, E.T. (1936) Unpublished letter to Ruth Woodhull Smith

SMITH, F.T. (1932) Some interesting animals of Szechwan. *Journal of the West China Border Research Society 5*:1–9

—— (1936) Letter to the Editor. *North China Daily News*: 6 December

—— (1937) Collecting a zoo in China. *Home and Empire*: 6

SOWERBY, A. DE C. (1936) The Chinese in the field of Scientific Exploration. *China Journal 24*:170–2

—— (1937) The natural history of west China. *China Journal 26*:202

—— (1938) The lure of the Giant Panda. *China Journal 28*:251–4

STAPF, O. (1904) On the fruit of *Melocanna bambusoides*, Trin., endospermless viviparous genus of Bambuseae. *Transactions of the Linnean Society of London (2, Botany) 6*:401–25

STEVENS, H. (1934) *Through Deep Defiles to Tibetan Uplands*. H.F. and G. Witherby, London: 198

STULLKEN, D.E. AND HIESTAND, W.A. (1953) An experimental study of the influence of pelage pigmentation on metabolic rate and its possible relationship to body temperature control and ecological distribution. *Ecology 34(3)*:610–13

T'AN, P-C. (1958) Animaux rares du zoo de Pékin. *Science et Nature 26*:9–11

TAGLE, D.A., MIYAMOTO, M.M., GOODMAN, M., HOFMANN, O., BRAUNITZER, G., GOELTENBOTH, G.R. AND JALANKE, H. (1988) Hemoglobin of pandas: Phylogenetic relationships of carnivores as ascertained by protein sequence data. *Naturwissenschaften 73(8)*:512–14

TAYLOR, A.H. AND QIN, Z. (1987) Culm dynamics and dry matter production of bamboos in the Tangjiahe giant panda reserves, Sichuan, China. *Journal of Applied Ecology 24(2)*:419–34

—— AND —— (1988a) Regeneration patterns in old grown *Abies-Betula* forests in the Wolong Natural Reserve, Sichuan, China. *Journal of Ecology 76(4)*:1204–18

—— AND —— (1988b) Regeneration from seed of *Sinarundinaria fangiana*, a bamboo, in the Wolong giant panda reserve, Sichuan, China. *American Journal of Botany 75(7)*:1065–73

—— AND —— (1989) Structure and composition of selectively cut and uncut *Abies-Tsuga* forest in Wolong Natural Reserve and implications for panda conservation in China. *Biological Conservation 47(2)*:83–108

THENIUS, E. (1979) Zur systematischen und phylogenetischen Stellung des Bambusbaren: *Ailuropoda melanoleuca* David (Carnivora, Mammalia). *Zeitschrift für Säugertierkunde 44(5)*:286–305

TEMPLETON, A.R. AND READ, B. (1983) The elimination of inbreeding depression in a captive herd of Speke's gazelle. In G.M. Schonewald-Cox, S.M. Chambers, B. MacBride and L. Thomas (eds) *Genetics and Conservation*:241–61

VEEKE, H. AND GLATSTON, A.R. (1980) Demographic study of the captive population of the red panda. In A.R. Glatston (ed.) *The Red or Lesser Panda Studbook No 1*. Stichting Koningklijke Rotterdamse Diergaard: 11–22

WANG, T-K. (1974) On the taxonomic status of species, geological distribution and evolutionary history of Ailuropoda. *Acta Zoologica Sinica 20(2)*:201

WATT, W.B. (1983) Adaptation at specific loci II. Demographic and biochemical elements in the maintenance of PGI polymorphism. *Genetics 103(4)*:691–724

WEN, Z. AND WANG, M. (1980) Giant pandas and bamboo. *Nature 1(1)*:12–15 (in Chinese)

WOODWARD, A. (1915) On the skull of an extinct carnivore related to *Aeluropus* from a cave in the ruby mines at Mogok, Burma, *Proceedings of the Zoological Society of London*: 425–8

WORLD WILDLIFE FUND (WWF) Press Release, 4 February 1987

WU, J. (1981) Brief history of research on the giant panda in Qinling. *Wildlife* 4:8–9 (in Chinese)

—— (1986) Giant panda in the Qinling Mountains. *Acta Zoologica Sinica 32(1)*:92–5

YONG, Y. (1981) The preliminary observations on giant panda in Foping Natural Reserve. *Wildlife* 4:10–16 (in Chinese)

YONZON, P.B. AND HUNTER, M.L. (1989) Ecological study of the red panda in the Nepal Himalaya (in press)

YOUNG, Q. (1983) Letter to editor of *The Smithsonian*

ZHU, C. AND LONG, Z. (1983) The vicissitudes of the giant panda. *Acta Zoologica Sinica 29(1)*:93–104 (in Chinese)

ZHU, J. AND LI, Y. (1980) *The Giant Panda*. Beijing Science Press, Beijing

—— AND MENG, Z. (1987) On the vocal behaviour during the oestrus period of the giant panda, *Ailuropoda melanoleuca. Acta Zoologica Sinica 33(3)*:285–92

Index